T0366012

Hope is My Daily Companion

Inspirational Readings for Living with Fibromyalgia

CAROLINE RHODE

iUniverse

HOPE IS MY DAILY COMPANION
INSPIRATIONAL READINGS FOR LIVING WITH FIBROMYALGIA

Copyright © 2021 Caroline Rhode.

All rights reserved. No part of this book may be used or reproduced by any means, graphic, electronic, or mechanical, including photocopying, recording, taping or by any information storage retrieval system without the written permission of the author except in the case of brief quotations embodied in critical articles and reviews.

iUniverse books may be ordered through booksellers or by contacting:

iUniverse
1663 Liberty Drive
Bloomington, IN 47403
www.iuniverse.com
844-349-9409

Because of the dynamic nature of the Internet, any web addresses or links contained in this book may have changed since publication and may no longer be valid. The views expressed in this work are solely those of the author and do not necessarily reflect the views of the publisher, and the publisher hereby disclaims any responsibility for them.

Cover design by Caroline Rhode
Interior design and images by Robert V. Welz II
Author image by Robert V. Welz II

Scripture quotations from the Holy Bible, King James Version (Authorized Version). First published in 1611. Quoted from the KJV Classic Reference Bible.

ISBN: 978-1-5320-9019-6 (sc)
ISBN: 978-1-5320-9020-2 (e)

Print information available on the last page.

iUniverse rev. date: 05/10/2021

To my children, whom I tried to hold loosely, giving you room to blossom in your own fashion. Thank you for your wisdom and the gift of knowing you.

Introduction

My goal for writing *Hope Is My Daily Companion* was to address the complexities that those of us living with a chronic illness (specifically fibromyalgia) face daily through offering new hope and concepts for seeing the joy in each day, despite having a chronic condition. If you are struggling with fibromyalgia or think you may have it or another chronic illness, I hope this book can help with the business of coping.

Some of the primary characteristics of fibromyalgia are widespread, chronic pain and stiffness without noticeable inflammation, unrelenting fatigue, concentration and memory problems, and nonrestorative sleep. Other conditions that may coexist are irritable bowel/bladder syndrome, temporomandibular joint disorder, and migraines or headaches. These are some of the most common of a kaleidoscope of symptoms that make up fibromyalgia, and they may come in any combination.

You might laugh or go, "For real?" so I won't mention how long it took to complete this book. I call this my miracle book. Although physical pain, fatigue, and the foggy brain we dub "fibro fog" are not a writer's friend, and despite having multiple chronic conditions—I persevered. Presently I am doing my best after years of being besieged with that knotty puzzle we call fibromyalgia.

Note to the Reader

There is no one way to use *Hope Is My Daily Companion*. It was written to help you discover the joy in the mundane, the beauty in the obscure, and humor in every day while living with chronic illness.

Begin with January 1 or the day you open the book. Even your birthday can be your first reading. Skip around, read it at a mere crawl, or gobble it up while you gain new insights concerning your fibromyalgia, or learn about this perplexing condition a friend or family member may have.

January 1

New Year's Day ... Today carve out a quiet interlude for
yourself in which to dream. Only dreams give birth to
change.
—Sarah Ban Breathnach

Let's be a little gentle on ourselves moving forward from today, for perhaps
it's our first year living with a fibromyalgia diagnosis, or maybe a decade.
Either way, we deserve a bit of coddling. We can locate a nice nook,
grab a favorite throw, curl up, and begin to indulge in various delightful
ponderings.

Let's put traditional resolutions aside, releasing us from the stronghold
of ordinariness into the vast world of dreams. We can start the first day of
the new year with a slow rhythm, like a waltz, and see where that leads as
we conceptually weave in and out with delight and wonder.

Our worst of days yesteryear may be our best forthcoming. The slate
is clean; we start anew, right any wrongs, heal shattered spirits, celebrate a
victory, or venture toward new quests. Let's relish our indulgent, timeless
musing as our minds spin skeins of nothingness, for far too soon it is time
to lay aside our meditative state, and as we launch into our day with a new
score stirring in our limbs, we rise.

Today is a glorious beginning
rife with change and opportunity.

January 2

Ask not that events should happen as you will, but let your will be that events should happen as they do, and you shall have peace.

—Epictetus

None of us asked for fibromyalgia, although now that we have a diagnosis, we have choices as to how we are going to cope with it. We may be wasting energy by struggling with our situation and wishing for the unattainable. This unrest serves only to keep the peace—and all the goodness that life offers—at a remote distance. Acceptance of what we cannot change (our diagnosis) can enable the serenity that is essential to initiate the healing process.

Living with a chronic condition can be more of a struggle if we maintain rigidity in our thinking. A sense of flowing with life instead of rowing upstream can produce a feeling of ease and comfort. This unfolding of *what is* may allow us to drop our oars now and then and simply *be*, introducing a modicum of peace.

I will pull up the shades of my discontent
and behold life in its essence.

January 3

Did you ever stop to think, and forget to start again?
—A. A. Milne

During our conversations, fibro fog may periodically rear its unwanted head. Whole areas of thought can disappear, along with vocabulary, expression, and speech cadence. Or the reverse, the weirdest things or combination of nonwords come tumbling out, to our dismay. It can be downright frustrating since the flow of our communication is broken while our brains frantically search for the word or subject we are discussing. Just thinking (an act that used to be so natural) is every so often an uphill battle.

When fibro fog pulls up a chair in conversations, it may be beneficial to finish the discussion at a subsequent date. Or we could use this "blank slate" instance to pause, giving the other person a chance to fill in the silence. This technique can be calming, releasing undue pressure, and enabling us to enjoy the opportunity to listen. We take comfort in the knowledge that fibro fog is temporary and that we will return to greater clarity. Let's savor those moments of eloquence when our words spill forth without effort and our minds are sharp once again.

I respond to my fibro fog confusion
with an encouraging attitude,
making tense situations more manageable.

January 4

Blessed are they that mourn: for they shall be comforted.
—Matthew 5:4

When we envision doves, we generally think of them nestled together. However, occasionally we may hear a plaintive cry of mourning doves calling one to another. Instead of seeking comfort together, the doves occupy separate trees. When in mourning, we as humans may find ourselves in similar seclusion and withdrawal.

There are many varieties of loss, from a decline in our physical condition and restrictions in our activities to the loss of a loved one or friend. Stages of grieving that can occur after learning of our diagnosis are comparable to mourning. During these intervals of melancholy, our previously healthy lives (the image of nestling doves) can be a gentle reminder to seek the support of a select few during that problematic phase of early diagnosis.

As I reach out of isolation and connect with others,
I hasten my recovery from loss.

January 5

At times of great stress it is especially necessary to achieve
a complete freeing of the muscles.

—Konstantin Stanislavsky

One of our most frequent symptoms may be muscle tightness. Our muscles
and tendons can quickly become stiff, and painful knots can form from
lactic acid buildup. There are several measures we can take to help relieve
this symptom.

Getting a massage by a therapeutic licensed massage practitioner
can smooth out those aches and is one of the pleasantest ways to relax
our muscles that tend to tighten even more during stressful situations.
We could contact a local massage school; they generally offer affordable
treatments. Or instead of a costly therapeutic massage, we can try self-
massage with a small water bottle or tennis ball. We can gently roll it over
the sensitive area, and freezing the water bottle achieves a cooling effect.

By alternating gentle tightening with relaxing each primary muscle
group, we can efficiently relieve some of the tension we hold; this can be
done sitting, lying down, or even while standing. We can then shake out
our arms separately, gently relaxing the muscles and repeating the exercise
with each leg. And afterward, we can relish a warm water soak, letting
our tensions dissolve as we immerse ourselves while moisture wraps us in
a welcoming, relaxing cocoon.

I will adopt a system to help free my muscles
from the viselike grip that pain and stress inflict.

January 6

But I'll know my song well before I start singin'
And it's a hard, it's a hard, it's a hard, and it's a hard,
It's a hard rain's a-gonna fall.

—Bob Dylan

When present hardships brought on by fibromyalgia seem to frustrate and dominate our thoughts, when isolation seems welcoming, before depression with its sinking feelings attaches itself, we can turn to acceptance as an alternative. There are healthier choices than taking to our beds every day. Seeking to generate daily interaction with others, even if for a brief encounter, can elevate descending moods, maintaining a balance in our off-center perspective.

Can we gracefully accept a fibromyalgia diagnosis? We wish to raise our voices, declaring, "This is too hard. I cannot do this." A lifetime of chronic illness is nonetheless a lifetime. This is more than some may enjoy, and for this, we can be grateful. We can sing our song of hardship for a time, but let's not get bogged down in it. Instead, we can become skilled at accepting what is, keeping depression from becoming our anthem.

I will learn a new song—a song of acceptance and solace.

January 7

The original lists were probably carved in stone and represented longer periods of time. They contained things like "Get More Clay. Make Better Oven."

—David Viscott

Today while out for a walk, a young mother with two children in tow came up behind me and said there was a sticky note stuck to my right pants leg. I had just paraded past several people with the paper attached to me! Glowing yellow against the black fabric, it was sure to be seen by all. It gave me a bit of a chuckle. Periodically, in my list-making fervor, I can be too hasty and misplace one or two sticky notes. I will have to check my clothes now before leaving the house. Fibro fog—always throwing me a curve.

We can spin our wheels by only thinking of desired achievements, although, if we do not put pen to paper, we may lose all if we are in a state of confusion. If we have never been list makers, it may take a while for it to become routine. Formulating notes can ease our fog, releasing the need to remember everything while shrinking the number of specifics we fail to recall. After a while, we can become more adept at listing our priorities as well as benefiting from the organizational skill of list making.

I can create a prioritized to-do list
and approach it gradually.

January 8

Learn to relax. Your body is precious, as it houses your mind and spirit. Inner peace begins with a relaxed body.
—Norman Vincent Peale

Tension held in our bodies does not depart easily, and it could take root, similar to a pine tree's taproot that is sent deep into the ground. Some might rationalize that there is no time for relaxation; this reasoning only encourages a further tightening of muscles.

The word *relax* is a calming word that slips from our mouths softly for a reason. We keep unnecessary hassle from arising as we pause for a time of respite, without forcing relaxation. One method of welcoming inner peace is by choosing an approach to unwinding that is appealing. A sense of satisfaction can arise from learning to take a break.

Research has shown we do best, have decreased discomfort, and are less fatigued when we are out of bed and active. Then, periodically throughout our day, we can sit and take a short breather, perhaps putting our feet up and doing nothing. Balancing our activities with leisure is our optimal goal.

There is always enough time for relaxation.

January 9

The facts of the present won't sit still for a portrait. They
are constantly vibrating, full of clutter and confusion.
——William MacNeile Dixon

We can face multiple difficulties when we are experiencing the confusion
labeled "fibro fog" when we attempt to communicate. Frustration may
abound when we try to grasp what an individual is saying. It may resemble
a complicated riddle crammed with words that seem to go in circles,
culminating with a stress reaction. Then the circle begins anew because
stress exacerbates fibro fog. It is not unusual to get irritable or feel helpless in
these symptomatic situations, for we may momentarily feel out of control.

Although the knowledge that confusion is temporary should calm
any possible anxiety, postponing discussions of a vital or complex issue
until a day when we are more focused (speaking and listening with more
clarity) can ease tensions. If a decision is required and we utilize the "How
important is it?" test, we may wish to ask for help with our quagmire. With
the realization that we will not be formulating a rash choice, we can then
relax.

I will take a breather when enveloped in fibro fog.

January 10

One must not let oneself be overwhelmed by sadness.
—Jackie Kennedy

Before our diagnosis, we may have led busy, responsible lives with demanding jobs or growing families. Physical activity may have been a given, and we were capable of significant achievements. Here in the present, we can recognize the fluctuations in our moods and abilities. And while we are preparing for potential changes, should we succumb to depression that lingers, contacting our health-care providers is the best course of action.

Physicians may suggest vitamin, herbal, or medical supplementation to help our symptoms, and we may opt for low-dose antidepressants to help with depression and pain. For some, drugs are not an option, so we muddle through the down junctures on our own.

Calling to mind the many happy moments can be a blessing and a means of offsetting the blue days. Let's try gathering a few personal remembrances and assembling a scrapbook. There's no particular equipment essential—just pictures on paper will do, keeping it easily accessible. When we encounter stumbling blocks, we can benefit from the positives in our lives by having a grateful heart. By acknowledging any sadness without lingering therein, we can move in the direction of wellness.

When sorrow finds its way into my life,
I can seek solace through happier memories.

January 11

Courage does not always roar. Sometimes courage is the small, quiet voice at the end of the day saying, "I will try again tomorrow."

—Mary Anne Radmacher

Diagnosis in our lives begins with a series of disappointments and to a varying degree, disabilities. Activities that were once effortless can be a struggle, and often, our attempts at the simplest of tasks can become overwhelmingly arduous. Having a conversation didn't require much thought prediagnosis, although, with fibro fog and other nagging symptoms, regular communication can repeatedly be laborious.

We may not think of ourselves as being courageous. We are handed a diagnosis and told there is no cure. Merely existing with those odds is an act of courage. Striving for a degree of normalcy by attempting daily walks and outings can boost our spirits and bring to the forefront our many achievements, no matter how insignificant they may appear to us. Nonetheless, by continually striving toward a better tomorrow and not giving up, we display an act of courage.

If not today, perhaps tomorrow!

January 12

Walk on a rainbow trail;
walk on a trail of song, and all about you will be beauty.
There is a way out of every dark mist, over a rainbow trail.
—Robert Motherwell

Be it a bad flare up of symptoms or severe weather, we can count on being stuck indoors or housebound briefly now and again. During these occurrences of decreased activity, it helps to let our imagination paint a picture of relief. We can welcome anything that makes our stay indoors more tolerable. Creative thoughts are an excellent source to elevate us from the dark mist of fibro fog, downward-spiraling dispositions, or a flare up.

Before beginning, if possible, let's turn on music that soothes and eases discomfort or imagine a favorite song or melody playing in our heads. We begin our journeys by easing into a relaxing chair and shutting our eyes. With the beauty of an imagined rainbow as our guide, we have a self-made trail of splendor; these are our journeys to fashion to our liking. Let's try imagining a path colored with soft pastels that whisper of loveliness and serenity guiding us along effortlessly. Or perchance we may decide vibrant shades of ascending hues are what we desire for our trail. After a while, we might find the shadow of pain and frustration that surrounded us dispelled and despair replaced with excellence.

By using my imagination to soothe and relax,
I will cope with the dark periods.

January 13

There is no medicine like hope,
no incentive so great,
and no tonic so powerful as expectation of something
tomorrow.

—Orison Swett Marden

Today we may be feeling dreadful and want to run away from the intensity of it all mentally. It is on such days that hope can swoop in, offering a comforting shoulder. Hope could be what inspires us in our many struggles, eliciting our pursuit of wellness. We may occasionally succumb to feelings of despair, and on such days, we can obtain comfort through actions such as prayer, or perhaps by calling a friend to inquire how *he or she* is doing or attending a support group.

We can hope tomorrow is a day that is ripe with improvements, one heading toward optimal health. This prevailingly positive attitude can preserve hopefulness. By doing something—anything—enthusiastic to distract ourselves, we can raise the emphasis from the unwell and onto the pleasant. Sustaining a moment-to-moment mentality, we know however dull any current moment may be, it will soon pass, leaving hopeful expectations in its stead, fostering a brighter tomorrow.

Hope is that delicious elixir I consume with pleasure.

January 14

I want to sing like the birds, not worrying about who hears or what they think.

—Rumi

Singing is a natural pain reliever, producing endorphins (the feel-good chemicals in our brains). We may be hesitant to sing if we are aware others are listening. It might feel like judgment or auditioning for a musical show and falling short. This may cause us to hesitate when we attempt to warble aloud. Our uncertainty can keep us from enjoying one of the most natural gifts we have—our singing voice. It isn't necessary to have perfect pitch to participate in the joyful creativity that is music. Perhaps feeling self-conscious, we may retreat in solitude to utter a trill. While engaged in singing, we might observe that problems and everyday worries become distant chatter.

We might purchase a karaoke machine (new or used) and experiment alone at first. Later we can invite someone to have fun singing along with us. When we are singing alone, with others in a choir, or with the youngsters in our family, we benefit the most from merely opening our hearts with a song.

I will sing
even in the uneven times,
for it is within these moments that I most profit from my warbling.

January 15

Start where you are. Use what you have. Do what you can.
—Arthur Ashe

We wake, we groan, and then perhaps we zone in on that severe aching that is pulling us out of sweet slumber. Some call it the "Run over by a Mack truck" feeling. Others say "Racked with pain" or "Run over by an eighteen-wheeler." Learning to accept it—but not dwell upon it—serves us well. Knowing we will not feel this way every morning helps us make it through these rough starts.

Remaining in bed for the day accentuates the negative. Since we know that arising will be an improvement, we can begin to move about after waking. Heading off for a warm shower or bath can soothe those aching muscles. Next we can do a few gentle stretches in preparation for our day's activity. Let's take a new approach in dealing with our discomfort by recognizing that remaining in one position for an extended period increases soreness. We can try limiting sitting to twenty minutes at a stretch and then alternating with five or more minutes of walking or other light physical activity. By acknowledging when we feel a rise in our pain levels and using our resources, we can hasten recovery and increase comfort.

I will do my best at this moment.

January 16

Advice is like the snow;
the softer it falls,
the longer it dwells upon,
and the deeper it sinks into, the mind.
—Samuel Taylor Coleridge

Any advice that is forcefully given to us will most likely face rejection despite its potential value. On the other hand, we are more prone to listen to suggestions when people treat us with respect and gentle honesty.

It seems a handful of people who haven't the slightest knowledge about fibromyalgia can be full of opinions, although they do not have any real familiarity with our condition. In this case, we can consider the source of the advice and murmur, "Hmmm," as a response.

Some of us may enjoy helping others with their difficulties, and if attempted in small doses, it can assist us in turn by offering a respite from our worries. Being cognizant of this, we can steer a conversation that would put the burden of someone else's decision back to them. Often people need someone to only listen—without solving their problems.

I am aware of the manner
in which I give or receive advice.

January 17

The camel, at the close of day
Kneels down upon the sandy plain
To have his burden lifted off,
And rest to gain.

—Anna Temple Whitney

Rest—it sounds so simple. But most of us have some degree of hardship with this blessed state. When we implement a nightly relaxation routine, we signal the body to rest. We can find an evening leisure activity that soothes us, whether it is reading a book, listening to calming music, or soaking in a warm bath. The repetition of our schedule signals approaching repose and supports sleep.

After sundown, light from technical devices such as a television or telephone interferes with melatonin production due to the blue light these devices emit. Blue light is the strongest light on the spectrum, and if it is viewed at night (through technology), our bodies get tricked into thinking they should wake instead of rest.

That often-elusive state of sleep is within reach. We can try writing down our thoughts in a journal or tablet at the close of each day; this can free us of anxiety before bedtime. The undertaking of scripting our concerns each evening helps ease any burdens, and we can then slumber in peace.

As I relax my body and mind, sleep will come.

January 18

I was taught very early that I would have to depend entirely
upon myself; that my future lay in my own hands.
                                            —Darius Ogden Mills

My parents both worked outside the home when I was a child. This meant
my siblings and I helped with the chores. Cooking was my favorite, and
for one so young, it seemed like an adventure. I became, for the most part,
the designated chef for a family of seven. Little did I know that years later
cooking would be this steep hill to climb daily.

For many, living with chronic medical issues causes a significant
reduction of our homemaking abilities. As we continue to achieve and
maintain our independence, motivation and empowerment are the
rewards. Let's not compare our present abilities to those we had before
we developed health challenges, for we can experience successes regarding
many activities.

When fatigue becomes overwhelming, we could perform a task that
allows us to sit. As we arrange our schedules to include our most challenging
tasks during peak energy times, we will create a more satisfying, productive
day. While we are savoring the intervals, we are independent of anyone's
assistance, and it becomes a lesson in self-reliance.

I am responsible for myself.

January 19

Adopting the right attitude can convert a negative stress into a positive one.

—Hans Selye

Are we dragging ourselves through the day stressed out, perhaps in mind as well as in body? Do we focus on insignificant details and issues that stir up problems and are best left unnoticed? It could be that we have added someone else's worries to our already burdened being.

We may have heard that there are two kinds of stress. The good type, otherwise known as eustress, improves and enhances our cognitive brain function. The bad, referred to as distress, can cause or increase many health conditions. Having as little negative (unhealthy) pressure as conceivable is our aim.

By turning our thoughts and actions into the enjoyable and positive, we release old habits and replace them with new, beneficial attitudes that lessen the negative tension that has taken root in our lives. We obtain continuing growth by recognizing an unfavorable pattern of behavior and taking the necessary steps to change.

Today I will turn negative stress into positive stress
by way of an improved attitude.

January 20

I cannot do everything,
but still I can do something;
and because I cannot do everything,
I will not refuse to do something I can do.
———Edward Everett Hale

An almost paralyzing effect can be present when we perceive something beyond our scope of limitations and become hesitant about whether to attempt it or pass. Our sense of what we can and cannot do can alter if perfectionism comes into play. However, to undertake any activity within our capabilities and not succeed can be better than not trying at all. If we attempt to accomplish everything, we are sure to miss the mark on a few endeavors.

Life throws many challenges into our path; some may be fitting for our participation, and we may gain immense satisfaction from even attempting them. Saying no to the whole lot and virtually pulling the covers over our heads can limit our growth. By maintaining flexible capabilities, we open the door to new active experiences and abilities.

With escalated fatigue and pain quantities, our abilities shift, and a modified pace is crucial to achieving balance. When faced with various challenges, we can move our focus toward tasks that generate positive, productive feelings. By keeping our goals within our "can do" range, we boost our self-confidence, while achieving therapeutic benefits.

I am conscious of my abilities
and look at challenges as possibilities.

January 21

Common sense and a sense of humor are the same thing,
moving at different speeds. A sense of humor is just
common sense, dancing.

—Clive James

What can we say has stayed the same about our sense of humor? Do we
notice we lack our light side now that fibromyalgia has been trying to call
the shots? Let's just add it back. That's right, we don't want to lose such
an asset to our lives. Humor helps to manage any random disparaging
thoughts and lessen that sometimes-awful pain.

Whether it is clipping comics, delighting in amusing jokes, or having
a joyous laugh alone or with a friend, humor is valuable. We also have
many occasions for a sense of fun while watching pets or children engaged
in play. Learning when not to take ourselves too seriously. Smiling and
relinquishing a problem are valuable traits.

When we indulge ourselves with regular belly laughs, we sweep away
sorrow and self-pity, replacing them with healthier thinking and living,
where joy becomes an ideal means of coping. Work is satisfactory, and
conversation is rewarding, but humor outshines them all.

I will dust off my dancing shoes
and allow my common sense to have some fun.

January 22

I have gout, asthma, and seven other maladies, but am otherwise very well.

—Sydney Smith

It is customary when greeted by a person and asked the question "How are you doing?" to answer "I am well" or words to that effect. It may seem like a falsehood to say we are well, but answering for our inner beings and emotional states, we may be well indeed. When we put our fibromyalgia symptoms aside momentarily, we can gaze inward for more clarity on why we are not sick at our core. Is it due to practicing meditation and praying daily? Or perhaps our feeling of wellness stems from having gratitude and thanksgiving for the capabilities we enjoy?

Just as light exercise and stretching can assist our outer bodies, allotting room for prayer, meditation, and worship can heal our inner selves. Chronic illness can be a drain upon our whole selves, body, mind, and spirit. The introduction of peace through meditation and prayer conveys harmony that creates a buffer from the often-hectic pace that we contend.

I may have fibromyalgia,
but my inner self is well.

January 23

When we blame, we give away our power.

—Greg Anderson

If we seem stuck in a blame cycle, we alone can change the settings, for it is a limited mode of achievement. Letting go and moving on are positive ways of being accountable. It is sometimes said, "I may be right, but am I happy?"

Some blame God for their health difficulties. Placing the responsibility for our illness on something bigger and stronger than we are may momentarily feel good, providing a source for our feelings. However, before long we will realize that God is not to blame.

When we have let go of any faultfinding, we are free to take ownership of our lives. By accepting responsibility, we start to release negative feelings. We can now embark on growing in a more productive direction. Not blaming anyone for what befalls us is freeing, health producing, and empowering.

Today I feel empowered by salubrious accountability.

January 24

In spite of illness, in spite even of the archenemy sorrow, one can remain alive long past the usual date of disintegration if one is unafraid of change, insatiable in intellectual curiosity, interested in big things, and happy in small ways.

—Edith Wharton

This illness, this syndrome, this condition we label fibromyalgia can get us down if we let it. We won't perish from it, but it could kill off any chance of having a productive life if we wallow in self-pity and are afraid of positive change.

There are many means of achieving a full, productive, and rewarding life, even when we are diagnosed with a challenging chronic condition. Keeping interested in whatever generates a smile or a feeling of accomplishment is one method. We can experience minor undertakings, such as reading up on the latest news, making us feel connected to other human beings while erasing the isolation factor. Additionally, enjoying whatever pleasures we can every day (however small and insignificant they may seem to others) might be the elixir needed to soothe and calm any anxiety about our perplexing illness.

I am not afraid of change
that can ease my burden of fibromyalgia.

January 25

Acceptance doesn't mean resignation; it means understanding that something is what it is and that there's got to be a way through it.

—Michael J. Fox

There are the days when we can breathe deeply and accept reality with an easygoing outlook or choose moodiness and irritability. As we ease into our day, we can begin unhurriedly with what is our actuality for this day. An appointment or outing may require rescheduling or canceling altogether as we become familiar with our energy levels. We can be mindful of not overextending the boundaries of our endurance, although we can benefit from daily moderate movement.

Later we may be up for a short walk, a few simple chores, or a limited amount of stretching, enjoying possibilities in each given moment. An Epsom salt, warm water soak may be in order, which often brings significant relief. Knowing that when we are experiencing a flare up we *will* improve offers a measure of tolerance and a method of coping. Treating ourselves with gentleness during a ramp-up of symptoms ensures we will bounce back quickly and regain our capacity to get on with our lives.

I can breathe in and accept this day,
this one day,
for what it is and nothing more.

January 26

In the depths of winter, I finally learned that within me
there lay an invincible summer.

—Albert Camus

Looking inward, what do we see? Do we gaze lovingly at our inner beauty?
Or do we sneak a peek and look away with loathing? Perhaps we are
somewhere between finding comfort and a relaxing warmth in our being.

The winter season can bring with it increased low moods, and a certain
gloom may begin to settle. Consider light box therapy, which is a tool for
seasonal affective disorder (depression in the winter). By impeding any
melancholy and elevating morning fatigue, we can then begin to emit a
sunnier disposition.

Through continually treating ourselves with the kindness and love we
deserve, we help maintain personal confidence and belief, for this is the
essence of acquiring that inner glow. Our wellness will be set in motion as
we continue to blossom like summer flowers.

Today I will acknowledge my radiant inner beauty.

January 27

Funny, I don't remember being absent-minded.

—Anonymous

Fibro fog with all its trials and follies can either be viewed with disdain and fear of permanent memory function or taken for what it is—the random coming and going of thoughts and memories. Some of our confusion may include difficulty recognizing people, remembering names, or using mathematics. We may even have trouble finding our way home! We can often become confused while speaking with or listening to others.

Fortunately, fibro fog is fleeting. Knowing this, we can keep it in perspective and, on occasion, have a little fun when it visits. We can try repeating some of the silly, mixed-up sayings that we come up with and chuckle at them ourselves. We can laugh alone or jot down our foibles to share with a friend later and have a rollicking belly laugh, taking the edge off this sometimes-dreaded symptom. A cheerful attitude lifts our day with gratitude for our often-lucid minds. Fibro fog is what we make it, good or bad, funny or solemn. We set the tone.

Today I will laugh at my fibro fog,
not allowing this sporadic symptom to gain undue importance.

January 28

When a small child, I thought that success spelled happiness. I was wrong, happiness is like a butterfly which appears and delights us for one brief moment, but soon flits away.

—Anna Pavlova

If we depend on our situations and surroundings to deliver happiness, we may be in for many disappointments. Sometimes when we are grappling with hardships, it seems as if the world and all our cheerfulness are suspended in time. Happiness is personal; it is entirely in our hands whether we feel joyful. A few approaches to achieving joy are through relaxation, meditation, and maintaining a healthy spiritual foundation, although it's okay to have some sorrow mingled in along the way.

The more we relish special moments and experience them for the gifts they are, the more comfortably life will unfold when we contend with opposition, urgency, or pain. We can gather images of selected happy occasions, storing them as recollections or jotting them in a journal for safekeeping. During hard times these memories function as a buffer. Happiness will then become something attainable, not just something hoped for.

I will create and own my happiness.

January 29

Time you enjoyed wasting is not wasted time.

—T.S. Elliot

Here's a novel idea—let's waste some time! We may find we fare better when we indulge now and again in this pastime called wasting time. An ideal day is one in which a portion is set aside for whatever we please, through ceasing activity and relaxing for a few minutes. Most of us are programmed to be productive, and it might take a few attempts before we can unwind without feeling guilt or an urge to be doing something every minute. Let's try for approximately fifteen to thirty minutes of daily relaxation progressing up to an hour. This can be a mood elevator.

By creating breaks in routines, we help lessen anxiety, allowing the remainder of our daily agendas to run smoothly. Along with relaxation, we can add worry-free fun and entertainment to our schedules. Leisure activities might include attending a matinee movie, visiting a craft fair, and window-shopping. Try jotting down a list of no-fuss interests to have on hand. Now we are primed for enjoyment.

I will approach life at a more leisurely pace.

January 30

We cannot control the direction of the wind, but maybe
we can adjust our sails.

—Fr. Emmerich Vogt

The ability to recognize our physical limits without overdoing it requires effort and practice on our part. Rather than running unchecked into the wind, we can manage far more efficiently by the gradual increase of our capabilities. It may serve us best to improve activities in increments—providing an adjustment to the modification period.

Let's make use of any skills highlighting our strengths while being attentive to our limitations and being prepared to readjust when necessary. Life gives us enough adversities. If we amplify our perceived capabilities and overexert ourselves, we can trigger further complications of our symptoms.

As we prioritize, focusing our energy where it is essential, the results can provide sufficient vigor for the enjoyment of life. A helpful practice is to formulate our efforts by recording our accomplishments and what we learn. When living seems to be all about challenges, we can look to our achievements for guidance.

I will adjust myself to the present moment,
releasing strain and averting overload.

January 31

We must cut our coat according to our cloth, and adapt ourselves to changing circumstances.

—W.R. Inge

As we often struggle with limitations, we may have doubts concerning the relief of symptoms like headaches. Later, after possible research and much prayer, we find head pain may be controlled or at least decreased through dietary measures, medication, environment (atmospheric pressure changes and allergies), and stress reduction. While we are busy celebrating this victory over one symptom, another may emerge.

We may have been experiencing pain with limited range of motion due to tendonitis, and subsequently, through great effort and discomfort, we move through to increased mobility, although intense aching may linger for a time. Then we say, "Thank you, God," and carry on. Presently, when we attempt to stand from a sitting position on the floor, our feet and legs may stop working as intended—and yet again, our pain can amplify.

Our lives require unceasing adaption to the waxing and waning of symptoms, as well as potentially deteriorating limitations. Learning to cope with grace and tranquility makes living with a chronic medical condition manageable.

Today I will be adaptable and will not grumble.

February 1

When we lose one blessing, another is often, most unexpectedly, given in its place."
—C.S. Lewis

Losses are never born with ease, and some of us may feel we have had more than our share. Good health, which most people name as a priority, can seem like a distant illusion. On this road riddled with health challenges, we conceivably have lost some friends along the way, although unexpectedly, we may have gained new ones in their place.

Some of us may have lost the ability to perform quality work or a favorite hobby; even volunteer work may be out of our grasp presently. Easing into acceptance of lost blessings is the beginning of healing from their demise. We can ask, "What gift has replaced my loss"? With the ever-changing hurdles we now encounter by shifting our attention to what is and not what has been, we can expand our coping abilities.

I will celebrate my many blessings.

February 2

If we had no winter, the spring would not be so pleasant:
if we did not sometimes taste of adversity,
prosperity would not be so welcome.

—Anne Bradstreet

There are occasions when I desire to live in a climate that has low humidity, a mild winter, and little precipitation. In such an atmosphere, I feel I would be relatively free of pain and fibro fog. Then I reflect on the dryness of such a climate and how that would affect my dry skin and eyes. Soon I remember the many attributes of my four seasons, and the emphasis on pain and confusion is in the past.

So often it is through our most challenging events that we learn and grow in strength and grace. Life events that we may long to undo may be the ones that educated us in profound ways.

A harsh winter season is similar to our fibro fog. We know it will pass and that clearer skies usually herald the return of our sunnier cognitive functioning. Ease in our discomfort can feel like a success. There is a richness of the soul and spirit, a parallel felt when we arrive at a temporary cessation of pain.

I will look for the silver lining
and grow in strength and grace.

February 3

The least movement is of importance to all nature. The entire ocean is affected by a pebble.

—Blaise Pascal

Body movement is essential for good health. We may be moving less and holding our bodies in a slumped position, which can trigger pain. It only requires a glance in the mirror on a day rife with pain to observe this in action. Perhaps we are involuntarily putting our bodies in a protective posture—shoulders forward and up toward our ears—which in turn could cause our heads to move forward, triggering overall painful constriction of muscles and possibly TMJ (temporomandibular joint or jaw dysfunction) difficulties. Let's relax and drop our shoulders, gently squeezing our shoulder blades together. Applying this posture while taking slow, relaxed breaths can ease tension.

Let's practice an exercise. Begin by shifting our weight evenly between both feet while slightly bending the knees. Next, start swaying gently, like a weeping willow in a breeze. With a gentle side-to-side motion, we alter our weight from right to left foot while moving our arms, keeping a fluid movement, remembering to keep it moderate. Just sway. We could turn on some music, cranking the entertainment up a notch and continuing to move to the beat. This practice can be done seated if necessary. Aim to do this for a few minutes daily. Now when we view ourselves in a mirror, most likely we will find our expression and posture have altered for the better. Freedom of movement assists us in lightening our attitudes and softening any edges.

I will move with some light activity today.
Adding music can transform exercise into recreation.

February 4

You live and learn. At any rate, you live.

—Douglas Adams

We often have to relearn a task, as even the simplest of projects might now and then elude us. Confusion may rule. Directions, recipes, instructions, math, and remembering names and faces are just a few on the daunting list of things with which we may grapple.

When we desire to retain information, discovering how to break things down into manageable pieces can help us cope. For instance, if we want to learn a poem or verse, we could make retaining the information more feasible if we reduce the task to one line at a time. If we don't put pressure on how long the process of learning will take, we can relax and enjoy the experience.

Let's set aside a puzzling problem until another time, leaving room in our schedules for enjoyable activities. By separating the achievable from the stressful, we approach living as a wellness tool that can ignite a spark of satisfaction in our day-to-day actions.

Today I will emphasize living.

February 5

To listen well is as powerful a means of communication
and influence as to talk well.

—John Marshall

Support groups are an excellent place to learn more about others by
listening to their stories. Although a meeting may have a "no talking about
the illness" rule, the opportunity for communicating and connecting with
others is a major plus.

One of our often-distressing symptoms—fibro fog—could disrupt
the natural flow of speech as well as interfering with listening and
comprehending. Perhaps it is in the recall that we lose the thread of what
was said, but we often do. After we have heard something, it might get lost
somewhere in the fog and come out altered, flawed, and different. Support
groups are opportunities to engage with people who are more aware of our
limitations.

We may come into a group mainly to engage with others who may
be having similar struggles and to learn how they get on with their lives
despite their limitations. Consider taking notes, including ideas that
resonate with us as we often come away with additional options for coping.
We can exchange personal information with a few we connected with and
perhaps arrange to meet again. When we share our feelings with a willing
person and in turn, listen, we can profit from the give-and-take atmosphere
that a support group affords.

I will listen to others and reap the benefits.

February 6

The way of progress is neither swift nor easy.
—Marie Curie

Three steps forward and two steps back is often the route we take with fibromyalgia. We may encounter a person who says, "Oh I had that, but I took such and such or did such and such, and now I don't have it anymore!" Perhaps this is true, but if there were a medical remedy for our condition, wouldn't this information make a medical journal, broadcast news, or a magazine article? The best we can do when confronted with skeptics is to continue to make progress no matter how seemingly trivial. The time and effort demanded to create headway in our recovery can be quite frustrating.

We can discuss any use of new herbals or over-the-counter supplementation with our physician. It is beneficial for us to have the support, advice, and counsel of someone who is schooled in medicine. And if we follow medical recommendations, we are less likely to have interactions or unwelcomed side effects with prescriptions or over-the-counter (OTC) products. We could keep a file with remedies we have tried and their results, informing our health-care team of side effects or unexpected outcomes when we have started a new medical or nutritional protocol. So while we dream of a cure, and attempt new therapies, we can be prudent and wise where our bodies are concerned.

I will work on my progress with a trusted,
qualified physician.

February 7

Turn your face to the sunshine and all the shadows fall
behind.

—Helen Keller

The temperature outdoors was 16° Fahrenheit. It was my last opportunity
to photograph snow before returning to the Deep South. I was living in
a subtropical climate when I undertook this trip. Arriving alone in New
York during the depths of winter turned into an adventure and a challenge.
The doorman said it was a bitter cold day, but what made it bearable was
the warmth of the sun. I meandered around Central Park for over an hour
captivated by the winter wonderland. My photographs were all blurred
because my hands were shaking from cold, but to me it was pure delight!

Our health problems and other worries are the shadows. The sun
might be kindness showed toward us when we are feeling down or even a
smile from a stranger. We can find our sun where we may, soak it up, and
let its restorative power pour through us. This attitude gives us hope and
focuses above and beyond a chronic condition.

For those who can tolerate sunshine, it is generally helpful (in
moderation) for most illnesses. We could try carving out an interval in any
season to seek a bit of sunlight. Being outdoors and turning our faces to the
rays can be soothing even if only to sit on a stoop or a fire escape. There
is something about the warmth of the sun that is comforting, especially
when our moods and health may be in shadow.

I will seek out the sun—
a soothing balm amid a cloudy future.

February 8

Laughter and tears are both responses to frustration and exhaustion ... I myself prefer to laugh, since there is less cleaning up to do afterward.

—Kurt Vonnegut Jr.

We may hear of people who went months, perhaps even years without shedding a tear; others cannot seem to make it through the day without sobbing. The act of crying when we are overburdened or in a flare up is one of nature's responses to our bodies' sensitivity to taxing information or pain. Crying can assist in releasing frustration or anger (inevitable in everyone's lives), providing a brief means of expressing flooding emotions.

Laugh with abandon. Have a good cry. Each is productive, although laughter is just more fun. Laughter can release positive, healing emotions, giving us welcome relief and aid in keeping things in perspective. By recognizing its healing properties and when practiced regularly, laughter is an agreeable reaction to life's little incidents. While exhaustion looms and frustration tugs at us, we can turn to humor to smooth the way.

I can cry a river or roll on the floor laughing;
both are healing.

February 9

Consistency is a jewel, but too much jewelry is vulgar.
—Evan Esar

It was winter, and I decided that soaking every day in a hot bath with Epsom salt would be comforting and offer pain relief. At first, it was effective, but later I developed a rash on my stomach from overdoing the salt soaks. My physician advised ceasing the Epsom salt until the rash healed. Soon I restarted the soaks, using warm water instead of hot and adding a few drops of essential oil to moisturize as I relaxed.

If we overdo anything, no matter how beneficial, the results may be unpleasant. Exercise, sleep, eating, meditation, and relaxation are healthy when done as recommended without going to extremes, which could trigger stress or pain. As we maintain a balance between consistent methods and the new and novel, we prevent boredom and depression from settling in.

When we assess our schedules and routines, we might discover we are shortchanging ourselves in one area and overwhelming ourselves in another. As we implement small changes in our lives, we can feel refreshed with encouraging growth, leaving unproductive patterns behind. Improvements, however minuscule, can shape our lives for the better.

With balance in my life, I gain a step toward wellness.

February 10

Worry a little bit every day and in a lifetime you will lose a couple of years. If something is wrong, fix it if you can. But train yourself not to worry. Worry never fixes anything.

—Mary Welsh Hemingway

Worrying could lead to anxiety, which can be very detrimental to our physical and mental wellbeing. A few may disregard the significant issues or thoughts of the future and fret instead over small, seemingly insignificant matters. Either one is counterproductive because our lives may include enough regular trials without increasing them.

We might consider our diets. Could they be contributing to any anxiety? As we tally our daily intake of caffeine and sugar or other stimulants that increase nervous tension, we could consider substituting caffeine-free beverages or foods and reducing our sugar intake. Decreasing or eliminating stimulants can be a calming, controllable option for maximum ease.

A fixable problem, when faced and conquered, can be encouraging. Or we could drop it and not address it until a later date, perhaps formulating a plan and course of direction committed to paper, instead of worrying relentlessly. Coping techniques require practice. By assuming an attitude of well-being and considering the damage worry causes our encumbered systems, we adopt healthier ways of managing.

I will fix it or drop it
when dealing with a troubling situation.

February 11

I've come to believe that all my past failure and frustration were actually laying the foundation for the understandings that have created the new level of living I now enjoy.
—Anthony Robbins

Several years ago, my ability to write or type was at a pause because of debilitating hand and arm pain. After much frustration and an inability to control the pain, I began a course of treatment on my arms and hands from a practitioner with an alternative approach, which was the catalyst to a healthy lifestyle change. I experienced reduced pain, which made writing and typing more comfortable, and I began daily exercises to strengthen them and protect them from injury.

Our lives changed when we received our diagnosis. We experience a myriad of symptoms and complications that can leave us frustrated, and our hope for the future may be dimmed further by the development of carpal tunnel syndrome or frequent tendonitis.

When our health takes a turn for the worse, we tend to reevaluate some of our previous decisions. This is an ideal stage for formulating a new wellness plan. Any outlook that provides us with successes is worth keeping. By thinking outside the box, we can seek the help of an alternative practitioner. We can begin to live with improved wellness and have a life filled with hope and an emphasis on accomplishments.

I look forward to living having a new understanding
of the word *hope*
and its effects on my wellness.

February 12

The eye of a human being is a microscope, which makes the world seem bigger than it really is.

—Kahlil Gibran

Sensory overload might leave us drained and irritable; it could also be a trigger for anxiety and headaches. The knowledge that we can experience a fibromyalgia symptom if we are in a brightly lit or noisy environment can assist us with coping. When we enter a facility with brilliant lighting or loud sounds, we may have the urge to flee. Chemical, herbal or perfume scents can also be distressing for some of us.

Carrying earplugs or cotton balls to filter the annoying sounds (yet allowing for conversation) could make the difference in a bad experience or a bearable and perhaps enjoyable one. While we are in excessively noisy environments (earplugs intact), we could record our thoughts or assemble a grocery list, thereby creating a quiet space.

Here are a few possibilities that could lessen the distress of our surroundings. Try a wireless music device that will allow us to listen to our choice of music (via headphones). We can slip on a pair of sunglasses and a sun visor (even indoors) when our eyes are sensitive to light. If necessary, we can use of a face mask or exit a toxic-smelling environment to breathe with ease. When our stimulated senses are calmed, we can then relax into a lighthearted conversation or remain comfortably quiet.

I will prepare in the event that
I encounter sensory overload in any form.

February 13

Be like the bird who, pausing in her flight awhile on boughs too slight, feels them give way beneath her, and yet sings, knowing she hath wings.

—Victor Hugo

Periodically I feel it might have been easier not to have ever had a diagnosis. I resisted getting a medical diagnosis for years because I was in denial. It seemed a few around me wanted the diagnosis for their conviction. After my fibromyalgia diagnosis, a magnifying glass seemed to be focused on my pain and other symptoms. I cannot undo the knowing; it's how I deal with the knowledge now that defines the limits of my misery or managing.

Friends seem to fall away like dry leaves in the wind once you own your illness. It seems a rare bird that can deal with all that comes with a chronic condition, and should we find a friend such as this, we can be thankful. If a person opens up about their chronic health condition, we may briefly share our diagnosis—or not. When meeting a new acquaintance who enjoys good health, we may consider postponing sharing information about our fibromyalgia diagnosis

We can find new friends after we have confirmation of what ails us. We should mourn our old friends briefly and then move on. Sheltering the information of our condition, like the fragile knowledge it is, might be the less-complicated route. Our former pals may stick around after diagnosis, and that is splendid. If they do not, that is okay too. New friendships are waiting to blossom.

I will dwell less on sickness and more on wellness.

February 14

Love cures people, both the ones who give it and the ones
who receive it.

—Dr. Karl Menniger

What a delight it is to love! With such a powerful emotion, we could soar to
new heights. However, some relationships sap our strength, making them
hardly seem worth the endeavor. At its best, the sweet gift of romantic
love can sing, causing all to shimmer, creating a slightly iridescent world.
Parental love can be more constant, unconditional, and unwavering, with
a relishing of the giving.

To love increases endorphins, which promote healing, making it a
healthy emotion for all. It appears that merely the giving of love should be
enough, but we want affection as well. Gaining the skill of loving without
overwhelming ourselves physically or mentally is a worthwhile venture.
Love can affect the hope we necessitate while surviving an incurable
condition, turning a mediocre life into a remarkable one.

I will welcome the giving and receiving of affection.

February 15

Even a clock that is not going is right twice a day.
—Polish proverb

Nothing guarantees that my brain and my mouth may be in sync, even though some days, I may concentrate more intensely. Today I called a family member by the wrong name. Next, I made an appointment by telephone with my physician, and I rattled off incorrect digits when asked for my phone number. Then off to the grocery store I went, and I had complications finding the correct street. Much later, my brain seemed to be in gear, and my fibro fog was a distant event.

If we are aware that we are having one of those days, we can release pressure on ourselves by letting go of the need to fight it. Our relaxation in the presence of stressful fibro fog is one way of coping with a symptom we cannot change. It is often difficult for family and friends to comprehend that our degree of forgetfulness and verbal mistakes (fibro fog) is one of our most perplexing symptoms. Knowing that stress can worsen fibro fog, we can practice stress reduction.

I will accept my fibro fog
and be gentle with myself when it occurs.

February 16

The most thoroughly wasted of all days is that on which
one has not laughed.

—Nicolas de Chamfort

While growing up, we might have been encouraged not to waste time.
Maybe we got the notion that most of our daytime should be spent
working—toiling. It may take effort to adapt to a different way of viewing
what we perceive as squandered time. We might see the unmade bed,
the pile of laundry, and numerous household tasks as areas to focus on
foremost.

What if we understood that to laugh every day is necessary for
optimum health, positioning it in the forefront in our day? Some of us
are so task-oriented that we may deny ourselves this healing tool. Let's
get serious about laughing; not only does it sound like fun, but it is also
a proven healer.

How then do we change a propensity for seriousness to one of laughter
and amusement? For some of us, it is as simple as laughing while watching a
cartoon or comedy. Reaching out to others with an amusing conversational
topic and perceiving the funniness in our actions and lives is an excellent
way to begin. What a terrific way of coping. Let's giggle, benefiting from
the freeing, lightening up, and superb relaxation advantages it yields.

I will get serious about finding the fun in my life
and roll with the laughter today.

February 17

We can complain because rose bushes have thorns, or
rejoice because thorn bushes have roses.

—Abraham Lincoln

Chronic illness can be taxing. Some have pain daily, in varying degrees, and
that could make for rough going at times. Everyone encounters hardships,
even the healthy; learning to take the bitter with the sweet is an advantage
when faced with challenging situations.

We might want to take a look at our bunch of roses. Did we get one
that had more thorns than flowers? Have all the petals dropped, and
we now grasp a handful of prickly branches? What may seem simple to
overlook when we are healthier now has a way of provoking tension when
we are struggling.

Once we have accepted our diagnosis (admittedly a thorn), we can
move forward with the rest of our lives. They can be abundant with joy
and laughter or could be maudlin and full of self-pity. Recognizing beauty
where possible is affirmative and health-producing. By exploring ways to
improve our outlooks and emphasizing the positive, we acquire an asset in
making it through a tough spell.

I will focus on my roses.

February 18

Until you value yourself, you will not value your time. Until you value your time, you will not do anything with it.

—M. Scott Peck

Our lives can be complicated. Carving out me time in our days is valuable and health-giving. We all have obligations, whether it is family, job, or households to maintain. How we use our time when we have completed that must-do list can be fraught with worry and discord, or we can lay aside our cares and fashion a worthwhile life. Our lives are ours. No one else gets to decide how we live and spend our time; we are free to make these decisions.

The intention is to create a fulfilling life for ourselves "in spite of" while discovering more about us. We all have that certain something that separates us from the crowd, even though we may not recognize it immediately. Over time we can acquire an appreciation for that exceptional flair or poise that is uniquely us—delighting in life in the process.

I will mold my life today into one that values me.

February 19

Laughter is wine for the soul—laughter soft, or loud and deep, tinged through with seriousness—the hilarious declaration made by man that life is worth living.
—Sean O'Casey

On the wall in her examining room, my physician has a framed quote that states in effect the doctor's job is to humor the patients while they heal. On a recent visit, I ventured to ask the medical assistant—in keeping with the sign—to tell me a joke, pointing to the sign. She knew a pretty good one. But it brought to my attention that healing was ultimately my job.

Every so often, we can get down in the dumps. It could be nothing in particular that triggers our despair—just the challenge of living with chronic illness. And then along comes something or someone that jumpstarts us back into living. Studies reveal when we introduce humor and joy to chronically ill patients, they improve in some shape or fashion. It isn't rocket science; one makes us feel worse, increasing symptoms, while the other calms and delights, leading to smiles and relaxation. It's a no-brainer—we pick the one that champions improvement.

Seeking opportunities to smile and laugh, which can boost our often-flagging spirits, is necessary if we are to go beyond merely existing. No natural healer is more attainable than pure, undiluted joy. We can choose to expand our lives with bright moments, transforming mere survival, into healthful living.

Today I will smile and enjoy a laugh, taking pleasure in
and profit from the result.

February 20

God speaks to all individuals through what happens to them moment by moment.

—J. P. DeCaussade

Flare ups bring an increase in pain, fatigue, and overall intensity of all our fibromyalgia symptoms. While overcome by a flare up of symptoms, we can take a few minutes to breathe deeply and just *be*. Not forcing anything, our minds may calm, and we may notice a release of pain—short-lived perhaps—but welcome nonetheless.

Living one day at a time may seem to suffice in general, although this approach can become inadequate on days with a flare up when everything seems to crawl achingly. One day at a time might appear to prolong our symptoms, and one moment at a time may become an effective method of coping.

Slowing our lives to a moment-by-moment approach can heighten appreciation for positives in our lives, putting aside the negative aspects of chronic medical issues. By pacing ourselves, we can recall the beautiful and excellent as a way of distracting ourselves when our days seem to be taken over by symptoms.

I will be open to my wonder-filled moments
as a valuable means of coping during a flare up.

February 21

O, there are voices of the past, links of a broken chain, wings that bear me back to times which cannot come again.

—Adelaide Procter

When we are first diagnosed, it may be a challenging period of dashed hopes and dreams and a plethora of conflicting emotions. We might be in a sort of shock. If we have a knowledgeable physician, we can begin our journeys toward wellness with an attitude of hope.

When we are trying to find health-care providers to guide us through the rough waters of chronic illness, we may experience a few false starts. We need teams that support our journeys from the "I'm so sick" mentality to the new chapters in our lives: "I'm okay." Physicians and possibly therapists are a portion of our support system; the balance is any friends and family who *understand* (or long to).

Letting go of what could have been and accepting what is now can enable us to continue productive lives—lives bursting with happiness and success with no bitterness toward what might have been. We are then able to proceed with an attitude of acceptance that welcomes healing.

Today I will be okay.

February 22

Sometimes our fate resembles a fruit tree in winter,
who would think that those branches would turn green
again and blossom, but we hope it, we know it.
                    —Johann Wolfgang von Goethe

Winter is a season of repose, awaiting inspiration from an outside source (or within) before we begin the sometimes long-awaited rejuvenation that ushers in the following season, spring. As we strive to keep depression (dormancy) from overtaking our spirits, it can help us to look to nature and the lesson we unearth there. During the frequent bleakness of winter, we apprehend that we will soon be graced with the budding of many spectacular trees, and this alone can give our lives something to anticipate.

We may pass through a winter of difficulties at any time, and the knowledge that there will be relief ahead helps us cope. To know with certainty that change will arrive in our burdened lives and to understand hardships will ease instills hope. And it is with this belief that we carry forth through the down times, looking ahead to the reprieve that we realize will follow.

I know my depression will change like the seasons.

February 23

People are never more insecure than when they become
obsessed with their fears at the expense of their dreams.
—Norman Cousins

Obsessing about our fears following our diagnosis can be a counterproductive activity. By fixating on our lack of health, we could force negativity to the forefront, which only hinders our wellbeing.

If preoccupation with our health is what defines us, we may consider seeking counseling to help weed out negativity. We can obtain guidelines on how to acknowledge our syndrome without it being our primary focus, thereby shrinking worrisome thoughts.

Let's pursue our dream careers and life plans, making adjustments along the way while factoring in our abilities. By extracting fear from the picture, we can focus on actively fulfilling goals in its stead. The recognition of our capabilities can firm up our wellness plans with choices that hold our illness in perspective while dreams are flourishing.

I will maintain a healthy balance between my health and my dreams,
boosting an optimistic attitude.

February 24

You are all you will ever have for certain.

—June Havoc

We can live alone contentedly. It is a viable option. Some of us may be alone when first diagnosed, and remaining in our solitary lifestyles could be our choice, and a healthy one for us to consider maintaining. For others, adjustments may be necessary because we've previously lived with family or friends. The changes and modifications we are facing may affect our families and could cause relationships to end or bend. They may not bear up under the burden that comes with a diagnosis.

Change is inevitable with chronic medical problems, and some loved ones may not be able to cope with witnessing the day-to-day pain and other symptoms that go along with our condition. Establishing healthy boundaries assists us in our living arrangements and the formulation of our life choices. Choosing to live alone can be rewarding and healing, and we may find we relish the independent lifestyle.

I will always be here for me.

February 25

No one grows old by living, only by losing interest in living.

—Marie Beynon Ray

Are we passing our time in bed or a comfortable couch, waiting for the day to close? We could be bored or frustrated about our loss of health or have lost interest in life to some degree. Turning our back on life does not mean life has given up on us. We can live our lives to the fullest within our present capabilities—regardless of our health issues.

Depression, a symptom of our condition, might cause some of us to have catastrophic thinking. Worrying only produces frowns and wrinkles; it never achieves anything productive. If we experience depression that continues over several months, a physician could assist with prescribing a low-dose antidepressant. Or we could take a natural approach and inquire about herbal or nutritional supplements, which can often improve fatigue.

Some ways we might consider staying interested in life are reading good news and sharing it with others. We can also telephone a friend to inquire about their well-being and perhaps arrange a get-together in the future. Let's try walking or sitting in the fresh air daily, which is known to have an uplifting effect on moods. By including smiles and laughter in our day, we welcome life and health-giving advantages, such as a decrease in the ever-present aging process.

I will maintain my interest in life.

February 26

A compliment is a gift, not to be thrown away carelessly,
unless you want to hurt the giver.

—Eleanor Hamilton

If the emphasis is placed only on our illness with all its complicated symptoms, we can sustain a weighty element. If we are in this mind-set, we may overlook a compliment, a small gift, or token given to us. These attempts to reach out to us by others are best when gratefully acknowledged, which can make for smoother interactions with others.

The ability to step out of our *dis*-ease and be open to compliments from our friends and family is a win-win situation. We may blanch when hearing, "You look so good," although accepting praise could be beneficial to all, generating good energy all around. The ease with which we acknowledge a compliment paves the way to receive more.

Additionally, we can deliver praise to another while enjoying the pure act of giving. Not expecting anything in return. We benefit from the opportunity of thinking outside our illness.

I will enjoy the giving,
I will enjoy the receiving,
and I will treat others with reciprocity.

February 27

Always be a first-rate version of yourself and not a second-rate version of someone else.

— Judy Garland

As children, many of us were placed into molds, whether by personality, race, financial status, appearance, and so on. Remaining in society's preordained pattern can hinder our growth and ability to develop into the unique person our Creator intended.

Through releasing these perceived limitations, we recognize that we have many choices in our lives. Even a life touched by illness need not be defined by it. We can discover our inner music. That which illuminates our true spirit could help us on days of flare ups and other complications. Keeping our own pace and finding our rhythm can assist us in de-stressing and unwinding, leading to a more relaxed disposition. By liberating ourselves from restrictions and stereotypes, we begin to step to our *inner music.*

I will keep pace with my music today,
be it a waltz or a rumba.

February 28

When from our better selves we have too long
Been parted by the hurrying world, and droop,
Sick of its business, of its pleasures tired,
How gracious, how benign, is Solitude.

—William Wordsworth

The world can at intervals be overwhelming; people and many inventions move us along at a dizzying, breakneck speed. We may be so caught up in the doing that we lose touch with ourselves. Sure, we might appear super productive when we are rushing along life's road at a brisk clip, although when we stop to catch our breath, we might not recognize the harried individuals we have become. It is often tempting to ramp up the speed when fatigue lifts, although maintaining an even tempo could be more productive, helping make sure we don't overdo it.

Recognizing the symptoms of overload and seeking a little solitude is a curative solution. We can establish a bit of quiet and retire with a cold cloth on our forehead and eyes. As we momentarily quiet the noise and relax our breathing, we begin to feel grounded and still. Before resuming the unruliness that life inevitably becomes, a period of tranquility can be effective for feelings of revitalization, renewal, and completion.

I welcome solitude—that precious state of nothingness.

March 1

It is important that you recognize your progress and take
pride in your accomplishments. Share your achievements
with others. Brag a little. The recognition and support of
those around you is nurturing.

—Rosemarie Rossetti

Those of us diagnosed with chronic illness may measure success differently
than other people. We are often pleased merely by rising, greeting the day,
and performing simple tasks. It can be a one-step-forward, two-steps-back
existence. However, if we only regard our lives with a black-and-white,
success-or-failure mind-set, our confidence may waver.

There could be days when we have something to crow about—when
moderate to high energy levels abound and achieving work, exercising, or
meeting with friends is achievable. If we are having an arduous day, we can
look at the smallest completed task as an achievement and reward ourselves
with the equivalent of a conceptual gold star!

We can bolster our confidence and self-esteem by continuing to
emphasize progress and successes instead of any conceived failures.
Learning to view ourselves gently can help identify our elusive strengths.
Did we manage to take a shower or bath? That is a success. Combing
our hair and getting dressed—one more success, and on our day goes.
The sharing of our accomplishments with a supportive friend can help us
recognize our small victories and pave the way for future endeavors.

I believe in myself,
and I can turn even the simplest of tasks
into a successful venture.

March 2

Language ... has created the word "loneliness" to express the pain of being alone. And it has created the word "solitude" to express the glory of being alone.

—Paul Tillich

Learning to enjoy being alone might be easy for some but challenging for others. When we become aware of our positive character traits, we can develop a sense of ease in our presence, so it is no longer a feared situation. We can launch periods of restorative solitude through recognizing our strengths as well as our weaknesses, leading to intentional self-discovery. Assembling a list of favorite things will provide us with further insight into who we are and what strengths we possess.

Spending significant periods of time by ourselves is time well spent. This interval can become an occasion for self-expression through prayer, meditation, or contemplation. When employing a daily measure of relaxation in solitude, we return recharged, refreshed, and able to generate improvement in our encounters with others. With the comfort we acquire through self-discovery, being unaccompanied is not to be feared.

Today I will schedule a portion of my day to be alone
and be enriched by my experience.

March 3

Happiness for the average person may be said to flow
largely from common sense—adapting one-self to
circumstances—and a sense of humor.

—Beatrice Lillie

We may be pleased to call common sense one of our strengths. However, it
may on occasion be disrupted by fibro fog with the realization that we are
not making *any* sense. Along with a generous amount of common sense, we
can benefit from welcoming levity into our day. Taking a lighter approach
to life's challenges reduces our anxiety. By applying the gift of humor, we
may find greater ease when adapting to our circumstances. Whether it is
confusion, pain, or one of a myriad of fibromyalgia woes, humor can offer
acceptance with hope.

There are certain blessed individuals whose sense of humor seems to
be their shining gift. Learning to incorporate wittiness into our day can
affect us constructively. The threefold balanced combination of common
sense, adjusting to circumstances, and a sense of humor can be the essence
of wellness. To accept and adapt to what life gives us is a practice in
lightening up.

Happiness is the balance of my good sense of humor
tempered with my common sense.

March 4

In any contest between power and patience, bet on patience.

—Lob Prescott

Life is like playing a game of chess; sometimes we find ourselves matched against someone or some activity that is larger, stronger, and quicker. But if we have ever participated in a game of chess, we know that patience is a key to advancing.

The strain and anxiety life can dole out may take a toll on our already maxed out nervous systems. If we succumb to impatience with ourselves or others, we can drift into the territory of an unpleasant attitude.

Managing chronic health issues can tax any relationship. And the people we encounter daily (including friends and family members) deserve tolerance, even when they do not always get our syndrome with its varied and complex symptoms. When we are compassionate and understanding with ourselves and others, acquiring patience can be a natural occurrence.

I will be kind and get acquainted with patience
until it becomes a true friend of mine.

March 5

And while we are on the subject of medication, you always
need to look at risk versus benefit.

—Temple Grandin

Physicians might prescribe drugs to help relieve our symptoms. We may
want to consider the side effects and interactions with other drugs or
herbals before beginning any pharmaceutical regimen. Informing our
health care teams of any herbal or OTC medications we are taking, as
well as prescriptions written by other physicians, ensures our safety and
wellbeing.

Treatments may claim victory over a symptom, but we may discover
it has a detrimental effect on our systems. There could be multiple
adjustments while we are becoming knowledgeable about pharmaceuticals
and selecting the best combination for our needs.

Then there are some who experience side effects so severe that
management options are slim. When learning to weigh the benefits versus
the reactions about a choice of regimens, some may opt out of drugs
entirely. There is no precise way to approach this personal aspect of our
condition; we are all individuals and react differently to various treatment
options.

I will explore the possible choices of medication,
their effects, and benefits regarding my symptoms.

March 6

He who knows he is a fool is not the biggest fool; he who knows he is confused is not in the worst confusion.
—Chuang Tzu

Recognition of the turmoil that fibro fog generates in our lives can lessen its periodic disabling effects. Through learning to reserve our more demanding tasks for occasions when this often troubling factor does not plague us, we alleviate a portion of our worries. When we are cognizant that we are experiencing confusion, we can work on reducing the tension that often accompanies this symptom.

The impact of fibro fog can soften as we recognize the blessings of days when we exhibit a sharper cognitive function, which could alter the perspective of our confusion. We ought never to feel foolish for occasionally misspeaking and misunderstanding, for these symptoms come and go. Frequently just a short break is all that is necessary to get back on track.

I will accept my fibro fog with poise.

March 7

When nothing seems to help, I go and look at a stonecutter
hammering away at his rock perhaps a hundred times
without as much as a crack showing in it. Yet at the
hundred and first blow it will split in two, and I know it
was not that blow that did it, but all that had gone before.
—Jacob Riis

Everyone is different, and methods that may succeed for one could be a
disappointment for another. As we learn of new supplements or stress-
relieving techniques, we can investigate to determine if there is value
in including it in our treatment plan. With our physician's and perhaps
nutritionist's guidance, we can plot a course of action to maintain optimum
wellness. Keeping a detailed journal of what supplements or medications
we have tried and their various outcomes could be of great assistance rather
than depending on memory, for we can get confused, and the facts might
get distorted now and again.

While continually exploring information about our condition, we
learn what could be beneficial, although this is often a trial-and-error
process. In our quest for improved health, we can remember to be gentle
with ourselves, without applying undue stress by hastening matters. We
can move forward in a relaxed manner, ever mindful to keep hope within
sight.

I will persist in my quest for wellness.

March 8

It is not necessary for eagles to be crows. What I am, I am.
—Sitting Bull

I stood in a superstore in front of a display of novelty coffee mugs and had fun reading the sayings printed on each one. After a few minutes, I had enjoyed several big laughs, some chuckles, and a profusion of smiles. Sometimes when I am shopping and frazzled, you can find me in the greeting card aisle, reading the funny selection of cards. This activity guarantees me several belly laughs. I love to laugh with abandon, whether anyone joins me or not, for this is who I am.

In the sheer work of struggling with chronic health changes, we may overlook the activities that bring pleasure into our existence. Recognizing our identity and our exclusive wholeness may be difficult for some of us. Our medical issues do not define who we are, and if we are unsuccessful in separating ourselves from our medical challenges, supportive friends and family can be valuable in encouraging our originality despite our many obstacles. They may have helpful suggestions that can be useful in a tedious period. Being accepted for who we are is especially gratifying.

I will acknowledge who I am today.

March 9

One sees great things from the valley, only small things
from the peak.

—G.K. Chesterton

For some struggling with a medical condition, this may resemble a steep mountain with our purpose (reaching wellness) being the peak. Others may view the journey as the aim. No one way is superior over the other.

Our decisions usually separate us into types. Some may give up without attempting to reach their goals or neglect to set aspirations. A challenging diagnosis can make it harder to see the bright side and our ability to recognize options may become diminished. Others may try one route or another, investigating every angle of our syndrome in pursuit of enhanced well-being.

There is no correct way to approach a medical verdict as baffling as ours. Wherever we are in our struggle, be it valley or peak, we can continue to explore alternatives to better our lives.

I will not quit my journey of renewed fitness.

March 10

I've discovered that I often visit the state of confusion and
find that I know my way around pretty well.
                                                    —Anonymous

Impatience can periodically reign over our serenity during cognitive mix-
ups from fibro fog. By relaxing and accepting when disorientation arrives,
our attitudes may improve. Fibro fog arrives as though an airline flight has
landed in our brains with a particular schedule and announces a layover
for an undetermined interval. If we have been here before, we know the
routine. The confusion will clear eventually, and this can help us cope.

Just as when we are traveling and encounter a delay, we bide our time
in our individual fashion, so it is with fibro fog. For those who are newly
diagnosed and just starting to experience this symptom, disorientation
may be unfamiliar. Adaptability helps us recognize the face of confusion
and even have a little fun when it appears. By keeping our expectations in
perspective, lightening up, and letting go of perfectionism, we can turn
upheaval into nothing more than a detour.

When confusion seeks to immobilize me,
I can utilize my flexibility by continuing forward.

March 11

Hope is some extraordinary spiritual grace that God gives
us to control our fears, not to oust them.
—Vincent McNabb

After a painful fall that left me with a severely sprained ankle (my fourth
within a few years), I had to depend on an assistive device for two weeks.
Painful tender points made it impossible to use crutches. I had no help.
Routine things like caring for my needs and preparing a meal became
enormous hurdles as it hurt my hands to propel the device. Despite these
obstacles, I had elevated hopes for a full recovery. After a program of
physical therapy, my ankle healed, and I was gratefully walking again.

Those of us with a fibromyalgia diagnosis may feel like lamenting,
"Whoa, this is enough; this is all I can handle." And occasionally, "This
is too much." But when we confront insurmountable disappointments,
a response of optimistic confidence is valuable. We can be amazingly
resourceful when challenged with all that arrives with our diagnosis (in
addition to the gumbo of frustrations that occur in anyone's life). When we
are stuck on the boat named *Distress*, we can use hope to row safely ashore.

I will invite hope into my daily life with fibromyalgia.

March 12

Sometimes the most important thing in a whole day is the
rest we take between two deep breaths.

—Etty Hillesum

To practice flowing during an uncomfortable situation is one form of
coping. When we are experiencing pain, it is an optimal occasion to apply
this coping method. Thinking about how much we ache only intensifies
our pain levels. We may not be able to stop the pain, but we can decrease
its adverse effects on us.

Let's try a relaxation exercise of lying down on the bed, a mat, or the
floor (whichever is most comfortable) with legs bent at the knees, feet flat
on the floor, and arms to our sides. Relax for about ten minutes. While
practicing this exercise, we may notice our thoughts dipping in and out
of topics. The more anxious we are, the more ideas seem to race through
our minds.

After a few minutes, we may perceive fewer racing thoughts or troubling
reflections, and a comfortable, calming sensation may emerge. We can do
this exercise with increased results if we remain awake while implementing
it. When we practice mind-freeing repose, we can enhance our well-being
by recognizing when our pain or anxiety has reached its maximum.

I will cope with my pain or anxiety
by performing a relaxation exercise.

March 13

You don't get to choose how you're going to die or when.
You can decide how you are going to live now.

—Joan Baez

Chronic pain can push us to the breaking point. There could be spells when it feels like things are too hard to go on. We may hear that fibromyalgia is a life sentence, not a death sentence. Knowing we may have a long road ahead may well encourage us to live our lives abundantly.

Here are some questions we can ponder:

- What can we do to exist to the fullest?
- Will we look back with regret or with a fondness on the lifetime we were grateful to have been given?
- What will we choose to do with this moment in our lives?

When we receive our diagnosis, putting everything on hold is not a practical solution. By focusing on the quality of the now, we don't merely endure but live our lives to the fullest. We have adjustments, some significant and some subtle. We get to choose to be as fit as possible at this moment. Let's aspire to hope and healing.

I will strive for a better life right now.

March 14

I like nonsense; it wakes up the brain cells. Fantasy is a
necessary ingredient of living, it's a way of looking at life
through the wrong end of a telescope. Which is what I do,
and that enables you to laugh at life's realities.

—Dr. Seuss

How can we introduce some silly into our days? If there is anyone who
would profit from feeling lighthearted, it is those of us with a chronic
medical condition. In this technically advanced world, to choose a more
creative organic form of expressing ourselves can be uplifting. Here are a
few ideas to get us started. We can render a dull chore on our to-do list
into an enjoyable, even fun task when we make use of colorful markers
for our list. Let's consider purchasing a coloring book for adults and enjoy
a relaxing, creative entertainment. Additional items, such as silly stickers
and colorful notepads, can bring anticipation and eagerness to our often-
lackluster lifestyles. We could add a happy label to our next letter or draw
smiley faces or hearts under our address. If we are purchasing stamps, we
can select those that stir our imagination in an uplifting manner.

Try this fun exercise. Choosing our favorite colored marker, let's begin
doodling a picture with our eyes closed. Then we can open them to the spectacle
of pure fantasy. There is no right way to do this. Merely enjoy the flow of the pen
and the artful results. Or we can switch the marker to our nondominant hand
and try drawing a picture of the sun or a flower or a giant smiley face. After
enjoying a few minutes of a creative fun activity, we may find our awareness of
our symptoms has diminished, leaving us beaming and refreshed.

By adding some fantasy to my life,
I provide a creative outlet for coping with my symptoms.

March 15

Develop an attitude of gratitude, and give thanks for everything that happens to you, knowing that every step forward is a step toward achieving something bigger and better than your current situation.

—Brian Tracy

Of late I have noticed a formerly impenetrable path down to the river has developed footholds in the packed earth and large rocks. This path is an area with a short descent to a cement platform overlooking the water that many people seek to view the passing current—and I would eye it longingly. When I felt I was experiencing a peak good day amid regular intervals of pain and fatigue, I attempted to reach that popular, sought-after viewing spot. To my surprise, I made it! Now occasionally, when I am feeling top-notch, I slowly descend, and while observing from this location with new eyes, I always give thanks and feel awash with gratitude for every step I take.

Often our abilities are so challenged that we shelve any thought of pursuing anything that we might attempt and fail. Sometimes we even find ourselves sinking into focusing on the troubling times. Walking can become limited, and when we encounter a period with freedom of movement where the pain is not at the forefront of our beings, it is uplifting to add a little something to our day. Be it exercise or engaging in relaxed conversation with others, tackling that once-undoable situation can be confidence-building and mood enriching. We can continually give thanks for our very days, whether they are pain or pleasure filled.

I will observe my bounty in life
by acknowledging more than my misfortunes.

March 16

In all affairs it's a healthy thing now and then to hang a question mark on the things you have long taken for granted.

—Bertrand Russell

Whether we only suspect we might have fibromyalgia, have been recently diagnosed, or have been diagnosed years ago, we may all have asked the following questions at some juncture about our condition.

- Do I have fibromyalgia?
- How long will I be ill?
- Will my symptoms worsen?
- How did I get fibromyalgia?
- Is there a cure?

We can address these questions and many more to a rheumatologist or a physician experienced in treating fibromyalgia. Preparing a small list of queries for the practitioner and making notes during the appointment could shed further light on our condition. Some illnesses can mimic symptoms of fibromyalgia, making it necessary to rule these out before coming to a definitive diagnosis.

I will seek answers from a knowledgeable source concerning my chronic illness.

March 17

Those who danced were thought to be quite insane by those who could not hear the music.

—Angela Monet

One St. Patrick's Day when I was healthier and my children were small, I decided to demonstrate how to dance an Irish jig—well, at least my version of the dance. I was humming a Celtic tune while barefoot on a hardwood floor and dancing with energetic élan when I landed on (and broke) my toe. I decided when I danced a jig again to wear shoes! It's a good thing my children did not follow my lead; it turns out an Irish jig is more complicated than I previously thought, and footwear would surely have been an asset.

There may be a stretch in our lives where we dance (literally or fugitively) to our own rhythm, and those around us may not always fathom our intent or follow our lead. Dance. Dance for the sheer purpose of being able to if only for a minute. Pause from a sitting task and have a two-minute dance party. Dance with only swaying arms. Dance if only in our minds. Dance alone. Dance with others. The benefits we glean from such an enjoyable activity far outweigh any disapproval we may receive.

I will keep hearing my music even if no one else does;
it may be intended only for me.

March 18

He who would learn to fly one day must first learn to
stand and walk and run and climb and dance; one cannot
fly into flying.

—Friedrich Nietzsche

One of the most challenging fallouts of prolonged health problems is losing
our former stride as we may have soared before health changes grounded
us. We are no longer flying, and it can sometimes feel like being grounded
indefinitely. When we were still very healthy, we might have been adept,
rushing through life, and skilled at various aerobic activities or sports, such
as tennis or biking. The loss of our former abilities can be a concern for
generating necessary adjustments.

When easing back into wellness, we may have to start from the
beginning, establishing methods to stand, sit, and move for reducing stress
on taxed muscles. If we are employing poor posture when standing and
walking, this habit could encourage our muscles to tighten painfully. Let's
try pacing ourselves as we begin to feel our way toward healthier abilities
through the basic activities we once took for granted. Walking is a terrific
exercise if it is not overdone. We can start gradually, stretching before and
after a stroll while increasing our distance in increments and identifying
our limit. When establishing our stride in our endeavors rather than
attempting to keep up with others, we realize enjoyable, beneficial activity.

By adopting a reasonable exercise program,
I will work toward wellness today

March 19

A successful man is one who can lay a firm foundation
with the bricks that others throw at him.
—Sidney Greenberg

We all try to evade the problems or bricks flying in our direction. Some may be from our childhoods, such as being teased or bullied. There could additionally have been difficulties that we could describe as traumatic. At some point in our lives, we may desire ultimate relief from any hardship or pain inflicted by others.

By remaining in a healthy relationship and exiting any toxic circumstance, we are demonstrating self-love. Enlisting a trusted friend or family member to help us leave an unhealthy existence may be less traumatic than attempting to depart without assistance. If there is no trusted person to help, we can go on our own, increasing our self-reliance and enhancing our wellbeing.

Through our diverse experiences, we have learned many lessons and still have more to learn. One of these lessons is to remove ourselves from the brick thrower's line of fire.

I choose to learn from my experiences.

March 20

Life shrinks or expands in proportion to one's courage.
—Anais Nin

Now and again during flare ups, the absence of a support group or understanding from a family member may leave us with a sensation of being alone on an island. Relying on others to guide us in our hope for relief from various symptoms can be disappointing. Having a balance in assistance from others and the courage to apply our resources could help with the management of medical issues while strengthening our sense of achievement and happiness.

By breaking free from any self-imposed isolation (which shrinks our perspective), we could reveal new vistas and feel new vigor. We can seek mettle within, guiding us away from seclusion and toward any degree of health-giving life. Claiming this simple act of courage could help recover a certain level of normalcy in our lives, lives that have been shifted and shattered to varying amounts by the debilitating effects of illness. And our existences can expand to the full, rich, creative ones that God intended.

I can be courageous by applying balance to my life.

March 21

The day the Lord created hope was probably the same day
He created Spring.

—Bernard Williams

Hearing a meadowlark's song and drinking in the fragrance of a dogwood tree in full bud are two indications spring has arrived. Spring, with all its expectations and promises, is akin to our hope for new scientific findings of fibromyalgia. We may desire swift discoveries from researchers concerning our condition, only to realize they are no closer to solving the complicated group of symptoms we face daily than they were years earlier.

It may seem as though some breakthrough is about to emerge. Then, just as a late snowfall comes and freezes off the tender buds, so it is with our syndrome. We continue to hope, although along with that hope, we toss on a sweater to protect us from the chilly air and await the coming of spring.

As seasons change,
I can hope for discoveries in research and treatment of fibromyalgia.

March 22

You can learn new things at any time in your life if you're willing to be a beginner. If you actually learn to like being a beginner, the whole world opens up to you.

—Barbara Sher

We can learn multitudes by watching a child or an animal tackle a new skill. They seem to focus on the results rather than the task, and the job appears to be done with reckless abandonment. With a zest of accomplishment, they view life as a series of events and items to conquer with rapt enjoyment.

While grappling with the often-befuddling fibro fog, we may think that *all* learning is now unobtainable and thereby lose our spirit for new achievements. It is never too late to begin again, to acquire a fresh talent, and discovering additional or renewed knowledge is always exciting. Let's resist putting pressure or results ahead of the gift of learning anything, at any pace. The outcome can increase confidence when selecting abilities within reason while considering limitations.

We can discover how to adapt and succeed in the face of altered physical and mental challenges, celebrating our victories—whatever they are. Our living skills could broaden as we face adjustment to the many changes that transpire, not focusing on what was but delighting in the new—while beginning again.

I welcome the opportunity to begin anew.

March 23

Why we are here is important, but to know where we are going is imperative. It's not what you've got, it's what you use, that makes a difference in how your life turns out.

—Zig Ziglar

Like a merry-go-round, many of us live with a routine that goes nowhere but back to the beginning. Many refer to this as being in a rut. It is relatively easy to arrive at this place of stagnation. We could ask, "What motivates us? Who motivates us?"

To have a plan is valuable. We may not stick to it, but at least we have one. Having a direction in our lives can produce healthful independence, perhaps bringing about adjustments previously not considered. While discovering our capabilities, we can get a sense of empowerment that is freeing.

Health and relationship issues can stimulate constructive progress where we have the opportunity to be cheerleaders for our own lives. If we are charting a course for ourselves (ever aware of our gifts) and profiting mentally, spiritually, or physically, we will have embarked on our journey, effecting a productive difference in our lives.

I will tap into my potential.

March 24

We do not believe in Rheumatism and true love until after
the first attack.

—Marie von Ebner-Eschenbach

Many useful articles and books have surfaced concerning fibromyalgia,
yet research has not agreed on the cause or made any scientific concrete
findings. No lab test assists in diagnosis. Hence, we refer to fibromyalgia
as a syndrome, not a disease. The fact that it is nonfatal is great news but
has perhaps slowed research even further.

We can go forth, adapting as necessary while maintaining a hopeful
attitude. Supporting our muscles through gentle stretching and participating
in moderate exercise several times a week can make the difference between
serious disability or enjoyed ability. Discovering that sweet spot between
a sedentary lifestyle or overdoing it physically encourages wellness. It can
be more beneficial to engage in gentle exercise every day than overdoing
it once a week or once a month.

Before our diagnosis, we may not have been cognizant of an illness
such as this. We learn the reality of our syndrome quickly and are grateful
for the abilities we enjoy. Our continual quest for relief of symptoms gives
us an active role in the discovery of new evidence concerning our condition
and a blueprint for improved health.

By learning about my chronic illness,
I replace hopelessness with knowledge.

March 25

The really frightening thing about middle age is the knowledge that you'll grow out of it.

—Doris Day

Age is not always a factor in our condition. For example, it is possible to receive a fibromyalgia diagnosis at an early age. Although the average age when diagnosed is midthirties, the effects of declining health issues at any age can be befuddling.

Welcoming events as they unfold and pacing ourselves in our tasks make for more manageable daily routines with less fatigue and hassle. We can expect some degree of slowing down as we age, and occasionally aging can be indistinguishable from specific symptoms. There is a common saying, "Growing old gracefully." No one wants to leap directly into it, so we settle into a comfortable pace and rhythm.

If it were not for a slower stride some days, we might not notice the delicate narcissus inching its way through the snow. Calmly strolling and taking in the sounds and sights is a pleasurable activity as well as a form of gentle exercise as we ease up—enveloping this moment.

Today I will note that for each day I am older,
I will gain a day of experience to my wisdom.

March 26

You have to take your little piece of the world that needs to be worked on and do the best you can, whatever it is … You have to start small, at the beginning, and that is yourself.

—Janet McCloud

Our abilities may have become altered because of chronic illness, although we should keep going even if we have a reduction in pace. With the changes we now face post-diagnosis, let's allow adequate time to reflect on who we are. We could adopt a new, improved method of looking within by balancing the reality of our desires with our abilities. It seems that we are often hardest on ourselves and may feel guilty without reason, which can become a stumbling block.

Let's devise a way of viewing ourselves that involves acceptance and forgiveness without comparing the present situation to our former healthy state. By loving ourselves, warts and all, we are in a good place to begin. By doing our best, we move forward with happy and peaceful hearts.

I can appreciate the joy in rediscovering myself.

March 27

Where there is no vision, the people perish ...
—Proverbs 29:18

Discovering our purpose in life may take the greater part of our existence. The pursuit of our niche could encompass many routes, although some may uncover their path early in life. While searching for God's fingerprints on our "map," we can realize that proceeding on our distinctive course is the best action.

We could create a journal of our dreams—our vision of what we may hope to accomplish. A good place to start might be with entries of our various jobs, abilities, and activities to date, noting the satisfaction derived from each. Next, we can move on to what we envision for our future: our hopes, dreams, and potential successes. Let's think on a grand scale, allowing for possibilities we may have never dreamed of. As long as we are moving forward and not turning around or checking our rearview mirror, progress ensues.

I thrive by keeping my visions alive.

March 28

Life is defined by time and seasons.
					—Lailah Gifty Akita

The seasons are an event in a circular motion. Spring, with its new growth and promises of mild days and beautiful blossoming trees, is indeed a delight to behold. Delicate shades of green replace the barren skeletons of trees, heralding the change of seasons once again.

What season are we in personally? Winter—resting, waiting? Spring—new opportunities? Summer—energetic warmth? Or autumn—transition, change? Do we perpetually cling to winter with its limited possibilities, or do we welcome positive growth and change in our lives? We can look for opportunities to expand and alter, returning to our true selves before we became ill—to something that produces pleasure.

I acknowledge where I am today
as a step toward where I would like to be.

March 29

You can discover more about a person in an hour of play than in a year of conversation.

—Plato

There is frequently a division of people into either the achievement-driven types or laid-back, easygoing individuals. Competitive games can bring out some aggressive behaviors in some, while others *play* games.

We often do not participate enough in the pure delight of entertainment because of pain and fatigue or other aggravating symptoms. Perhaps we equate playing with only the young. Amusement can be an enjoyable coping aid when our moods are dismal. Let's try tucking a heating pad behind our backs (if needed), grabbing a snack, propping up our feet, and occupying ourselves while enjoying this pastime.

We are never too old to engage in games where we relax into laughing and delighting in the entertainment by ourselves or with another. Having fun, in any capacity, keeps aging and frowns from owning our expressions. Smiles appear, and laughter tumbles around like dandelions drifting in the breeze.

I will rediscover my lighter side
by indulging in a playful activity today.

March 30

If you nurture your mind, body, and spirit, your time will expand. You will gain a new perspective that will allow you to accomplish much more.

—Brian Koslow

Chronic medical issues as a result of fibromyalgia doesn't mean our days are numbered, and although there may be adjustments to our quality of life, there is always something to be accomplished even when we are feeling out of sorts. Having a day when walking is too problematic produces an opportunity for us to catch up on a little correspondence that we have been postponing.

Perhaps on another occasion when we may be experiencing fibro fog, this can be a convenient time to take a cleansing walk. By freeing our minds from all the clutter they attract and drinking in our natural surroundings we replenish our spirits and strengthen our bodies. This nurturing can usher in a new perspective whereby we could feel a sense of renewal and awakening of a dormant healthy frame of mind—where progress becomes a possibility.

I will nurture my mind, body, and spirit
while reaping the rewards.

March 31

Disappointments are to the soul what the thunderstorm
is to the air.
                                    —Friedrich von Schiller

Encountering a severe weather pattern with its intensity, chaos, and
confusion is akin to the effects of disappointments concerning our
expectations. Not knowing where lightning will strike next or if the rain
or wind will increase might be unsettling and even frightening at times.
Frustration when we encounter setbacks could leave a trail (debris of
discontent) that can dispel the setting of realistic goals for ourselves.

In the depths of a storm, as in the sorrow of disappointment, we can
rely on the insight, "This too, shall pass." The day after a storm can be
sunny and relatively calm. It is like a day with frustrations—everything
could be serene by the following morning. Anxiety and stress can be held
in check when we prioritize and work on reducing our difficulties. By
keeping our problems in perspective, we can turn the severe thunderstorm
of our emotions into a nurturing spring shower.

Disappointments are part of my life,
but they are not the principal focus of my day.

April 1

You can't be afraid of what people will say. You have to be
brave and take risks.

—Charles M. Schulz

We probably know of someone—perhaps we are even a bit this way—
whose decisions may come with the question, "What will people think?"
Overemphasis on how others may be judging or viewing us can spin into
self-involvement. Generally, most folks are just not thinking about us that
much. Whew, what a relief. To live a life with this unnecessary burden is
akin to trying to swim while carrying a bowling ball. Why would we want
to do this? We can drop that ball of self-judgment and focus instead on
what to accomplish with our newfound freedom from worry.

Being brave in the face of an occasional stare, whisper, or downright
insulting laugh may sound unmanageable. However, our ability to chuckle
at our *own* mistakes, confusion, fumbles, and occasionally unsteady gait
while minimizing tension and taking a bite out of what others do or say is
valuable. Then, bravery becomes a reality.

I will free my fearful thoughts for affirmative action.

April 2

Are anybody's parents typical?

—Madeleine L'Engle

Many years ago (before my fibromyalgia diagnosis) when my symptoms were coming at me right and left, and no one seemed to be able to figure out the cause, my mother lacked understanding or compassion. I cannot say this did not hurt, but I tried not to dwell upon it. Fibromyalgia was unknown in the general population. Fast forward many years later, and my mother ordered a book about my condition and read it before she gave it to me. She ceased her negativity, and I was amazed at her change of heart.

It must be difficult as a parent to have a child (of any age) with fibromyalgia. I cannot imagine, as the desire to help yet still give us our dignity must be challenging. If we have parents who are trying to navigate the obstacle-filled waters of our chronic condition while having to care for themselves and perhaps other family members, we can give them an overdue thanks.

Sometimes well-meaning parents do not always know how to deal with something as perplexing as fibromyalgia. It may cause fear in some, and they may retreat because of their helplessness or feelings of their immortality. The inability to fix us can perhaps be off-putting. Patience and love can go a long way when communicating with our families.

I will not put undue emphasis on anything
my parents did or did not do
about understanding my condition.

April 3

I truly believe that the boredom of illness is perilous to
one's health.

—Tyne O'Connell

If we are approaching our days with dread and boredom, we can quickly
slide into a rut that may bring on self-pity concerning our health—or lack
thereof. Let's try living each day as it arrives, observing the changes in our
lives. We have only this one life, and making the most of it is a challenge
worth pursuing.

Why not dare to seek something new and different today, even if the
beginning is small? Maybe it will be taking an impromptu walk or riding
in a vehicle with no goal in mind except soaking up the day. Let's start
that garden—enjoying every aspect of its growth with visions of flowers
or vegetables and relishing each step of the process. Or we can assemble a
keepsake for a friend or a child with photographs taken of them through
the years and gifting for a milestone achievement or no special occasion.
Most of all, we might realize that what time we do have can be spent
excellently.

I am grateful for this moment in time,
and I will enjoy it with spontaneity and happiness.

April 4

Insomnia is a gross feeder. It will nourish itself on any
kind of thinking, including thinking about not thinking.
                                        —Clifton Fadiman

Chances are on many a night we lie in bed, thoughts spinning, unable to
sleep. We may then attempt to concentrate on not thinking, which might
quickly morph musing into worrying. Flowing ideas can be welcomed
during our waking hours, although when we try to sleep while we are
processing information, it could progress into a fretful, sleepless night.

When our thoughts are churning, we can reach for a pad of paper and
pen that we can store at our bedside and jot our reflections down. Perhaps
we have ideas for a project or a specific goal. Making short notations while
they are fresh can aid in any recollection glitches. Keeping these notes
succinct diminishes further stimulation of our brains before we sleep.

Having emptied our mind chatter, we can now attempt to sleep once
again. Now let's focus our attention solely on our breathing, beginning
with a breath that inflates the abdomen slightly and deflates on the out
breath (with a whoosh of air). After completing about ten of these belly
breaths—we may never reach ten—sleep could envelop us. We can benefit
from the gift of slumber when our minds cease churning with thoughts.

I will record my bedtime mental chatter,
clearing the way for repose.

April 5

The grand essentials of happiness are: something to do,
something to love, and something to hope for.
                                    —Joseph Addison

Before any chronic illness strikes, we tend not to dwell on happiness; it
is just there, perhaps even taken for granted. After diagnosis, we may
frequently have to strive to achieve levels of joy and pleasure that were a
given previously. The limitations of our condition might present us with
more significant challenges, but there is always something within our
abilities that we can enjoy.

For example, if we love cooking, signing up for a cooking class could be
an option. This informal interaction with others where everyone attempts
to grasp something new can foster lighthearted, fun-filled moments. Or if
we are unable to attend classes, viewing a cooking show on television while
following along with the recipe can be fun. Don't have the ingredients?
No worries. We can enjoy observing the food preparation while making
notes (if interested) to visit later. It's not about creating a perfect soufflé
as much as moments spent enjoying the process. The list of activities that
are still within our grasp is endless; pick one and delight in the process.

Happiness—I will try it on today.

April 6

Reflect upon your present blessings, of which every man has many: not on your past misfortunes of which all men have some.

—Charles Dickens

When we reflect upon our past, some upsetting incidents may come to light. If we find ourselves dwelling on these negative occurrences, we can make a list of our blessings, bringing the constructive to light. By starting with favorite family members, friends, and pets, advancing to all that we are presently grateful for in our lives, most of us could compose this list with little effort.

Bringing the encouraging aspects of our lives into focus is worthwhile, especially when painful symptoms envelop us. If we are losing sight of our blessings, referring to our notations can spark a smile as gifts we are blessed with are acknowledged. Then we can leave past misfortunes where they belong—in the past. Enjoying fond memories of yesterday while living in and thinking on today is a recipe for increased wellness.

I will make notations of my blessings today,
keeping them at hand.

April 7

The words "I am ..." are potent words; be careful what you hitch them to. The thing you're claiming has a way of reaching back and claiming you.

—A.L. Kitselman

We might go through our days saying, "I am sick ... I have fibromyalgia" or "I am chronically ill." Even though these might be correct statements, bringing them up regularly can make others uncomfortable and do nothing to improve our well-being. How do we find a balance between denying a chronic illness diagnosis and emphasizing our condition?

Let's try to attend a support fellowship to bond without having to explain our illness because they "get us." Members of support groups can be understanding and helpful while they similarly cope with the whole gamut of problems that come with our diagnosis. Some groups discourage mentioning illness; the mind-set is to get the participants to move out of any sick-thinking mentality.

It is worthy of an attempt to discontinue fixating on and making references to the fact that we have a debilitating condition. People will find it easier to be in our presence when we reserve any moaning and groaning for our journals, allotting positive energy for living.

I am foremost a person, above all other things.

April 8

To me, faith means not worrying.

—John Dewey

There are multitudes of issues that could ensnare us in a worry cycle. We may be conscious of the havoc that obsessive worrying causes in our daily efforts for health and well-being—yet breaking this agonizing cycle can be challenging. Along with stress and anxiety, our pain levels may ramp up from continual fretting.

Sleep can often become elusive when we lay there worrying, spinning our wheels, and getting nowhere but anxious. When our heads hit the pillow, we could be in this futile pattern of replaying our entire day or planning out the next. Rethinking what was and prethinking what might be offers a scant solution. Even relaxation exercises cease to help if we then take the problems back after a few minutes.

In our efforts to stop this mental merry-go-round, we may resort to sleep medications or lose necessary sleep. There is a simpler approach to the conundrum. We can tap into our spirituality and let it pour into our very bones. Polishing our beliefs and turning everything over to God is freeing.

By ceasing to worry, I acknowledge my faith.

April 9

Believe in yourself and what you feel. Your power will come from that.

—Melissa Etheridge

Making essential telephone calls, paying current bills, and shopping for groceries may seem insignificant accomplishments to others. But for those with diminished health capacities, they can feel like major achievements. After completing our to-do lists, we are free to concentrate on the want-to-do lists, including activities that contribute to our general well-being and happiness.

Projects we hope to start or continue, in addition to interesting places we wish to visit, can each become realities when we adopt faith in ourselves and our abilities. Perhaps we have been considering painting lessons, attending gentle exercise classes, or visiting an aquarium or farmer's market. Let's try putting aside our chronic condition and everything that comes with it—the endless physician visits and often many pills to swallow—and search for the person inside these medical challenges. Recognizing our skills and harnessing them is empowering. Believing will get us halfway there; the rest is all downhill.

I believe in my ability to achieve.

April 10

The ability to be in the present moment is a major component of mental wellness.

—Abraham Maslow

We may find ourselves projecting a "what-if" type of thinking where we retain nothing of value; it is often only anxiety-producing. This kind of thought pattern might be unintentional. We could find ourselves drifting into a daydream of what our lives would be like without a diagnosis of a chronic illness. If our current moment is a burden of worry, let's engage in a few slow, deep, cleansing breaths, releasing any troubling thoughts or judgments.

Our symptoms are a constant shifting of flare ups and remissions, a series of agreeable events, perhaps followed by challenging symptoms. Seizing those quality times and expanding their duration can be strengthening. By limiting our emphasis on negatives and finding the positives in the present, we can benefit from the calm of living in the now. As we look neither forward nor backward but stay rooted here in the present, we encourage wellness.

I will live this one day, moment by moment.

April 11

Nice how we never get dizzy from doing good turns.
—George Bengis

Because of symptoms of fibromyalgia, most of us have faced occasions when relying on others for assistance was necessary. Although when we are able, we can look for opportunities to extend our help to someone in need. A few of the benefits when we help people are feeling a connection with another, an improved sense of well-being, and increased happiness.

Some ideas for assisting others can include visiting an elderly neighbor or a local retirement facility. Perhaps volunteering our time at a place of worship speaks to us. Reaching out by telephone to a family member inquiring about *his or her* health (without mentioning our woes) doesn't require leaving home. And we could consider inviting a friend to lunch who has been there for us repeatedly while keeping the conversation light and uplifting, inquiring about how they are feeling and if asked how we are faring, focusing on the positives. When we, in turn, assist others, we demonstrate gratitude toward those who have supported us in the past.

I give the most
when I share what is most precious to me—my time.

April 12

The black ink of anxiety spilled and spread, saturating the
fabric of my life.
—Eileen Simpson

Often the events that create the most anxiety are those that are out of our
control. Anxiety can seep into the core of our lives, wreaking havoc if we
allow this reaction to people or difficulties to take root. Attempting to
control the uncontrollable is an indication we are hanging out the welcome
sign for unease. By maintaining a healthy distance from taxing situations,
we practice health-inducing techniques. Detaching from an unhealthy
situation or an unreasonable individual can be in our best interest.

If we feel anxiety creeping in or swooping down, we can remove
ourselves from the situation and begin slow, healing breaths. In some cases,
if we are unable to leave a tense encounter immediately, a soothing coping
choice is mentally reciting a preferred prayer, poem, or song lyric. There is
nothing beneficial about anxiety; by learning how to respond to stressful
situations, we improve our welfare.

At the first sign of anxiety,
I will practice a healing, coping technique.

April 13

A single event can awaken within us a stranger totally unknown to us.

—Antione de Saint-Exupery

What can inhibit some from making a change that would be a welcome? Could it be we are comfortable with the familiar and fear of the unknown may hinder us from trying anything new? Additionally, we might often ponder the query of what would someone else do in our situation. By not comparing ourselves to others, we are free to pursue our dreams, blaze a new path, and focus on our willingness to make small or more substantial changes.

On occasion, it might take an event of sizeable proportions to jolt us out of sameness and into decisive change. Reluctance to face the unfamiliar in our lives is maybe the most noteworthy game-changer we confront. By conquering the essential as well as the superfluous, tweaking things here and there, we adapt to new challenges and variations. And by putting aside any reservations and trying fresh ideas while going after our dreams, we awaken our enchanting spirit within.

I can make a change today even a subtle one for my benefit alone.

April 14

Bad habits are like chains that are too light to feel until they are too heavy to carry.

—Warren Buffet

Sleeping the fitful sleep of the chocolate-riddled brain, I awake irritable, restless, and moody. I denied myself the indulgence of chocolate (I tested hypersensitive) for quite a while; however, after adhering to such a wholesome lifestyle, I felt deprived and overindulged, paying the consequences.

Compared to most, we frequently have an increase in food allergies and sensitivities. On occasion, it may be tough to turn away from tempting fare. By indulging in a small taste of the "forbidden" food, we can ease what could become an unhealthy habit to merely a side-step. We can weigh the side effects of nutrients we are sensitive to with the pleasure factor. Is it a bad habit to splurge now and then—in moderation? Probably not. Adhering to a diet that has many restrictions can be taxing. Allowing for room to indulge now and then merely makes us human.

My life is fraught with cannot do and cannot have.
I will occasionally consider lifting a restriction.

April 15

When one door closes, another opens. But we often look so regretfully upon the closed door that we don't see the one that opened for us.

—Alexander Graham Bell

Regrets are familiar to those of us with medical challenges. We lose friends, loved ones, and physical abilities. Staying optimistic while beset with regrets can be challenging.

When we are facing a door that appears to be closing, here are a couple of questions we may ask ourselves: Who is doing the closing? Is it our doing? Are we burning our bridges? As our struggles with the ever-changing effects of a health diagnosis mount, it is advantageous to view these challenges with an open mind.

An open door presents itself as an opportunity, a welcome sign. To walk away from a lifestyle, activity, place, or person may at first seem unfeasible, although it may only be by acceptance of our current situation whereby we perceive another route. Peek inside that open door; we may be surprised to find ourselves with health as our goal and our self-respect restored.

I will approach my open door without regrets.

April 16

Only action gives life strength; only moderation gives it charm.

—Jean Paul Richter

Midway between a sedentary existence and running ten miles a day lays a modest and obtainable activity level for us. Finding our comfort zone while enabling our bodies to get the exercise they crave for optimal wellness could take time and patience. It is often hit and miss when it comes to choosing an activity. Learning to find that balance might sometimes be trickier than anticipated. We learn that running footraces is hardly something to aim for, yet excessive relaxation can bring about increased pain.

Maintaining a healthy approach to exercise/stretching without overdoing it can be a challenge for us. Swimming (in warm water) is a known beneficial form of working out, but when we think of actual swimming, our response might be, "No way!" Merely walking in water, feeling a resistance not felt on land, provides an increase in muscle strengthening while the warmth of the water diffuses any pain.

Through trial and error, we can realize the best possible form of activity geared to individual requirements and approached in increments. When we remain inside our physical limits, we treat our bodies with care.

I will begin a personal exercise routine today
that is scaled to my present abilities.

April 17

There is a time that we must firmly choose the course we will follow, or the relentless drift of events will make the decision for us.

—Herbert B. Prochnow

Receiving a fibromyalgia diagnosis can be an event that will change (in varying degrees) the course of our lives. Our lives to date have consisted of many ups and downs as a result of our decisions and the outcome of our choices. Some of these decisions may have set us back, while others may have empowered us with strength and control. A recent diagnosis may have affected our lives and altered, to some extent, our decision-making.

We can choose a new path, one that is not defined by fibromyalgia, but that is undoubtedly affected by this chronic condition. Our wellness is under our control as we formulate decisions and choices concerning our health and well-being. It is easy for us to sit back, letting the day drift by and pretending that nothing has changed. But it has. We do best when we accept the reality of our situation and remain in control while mapping out a health plan.

I am in control of my life decisions.

April 18

Consult not your fears but your hopes and your dreams. Think not about your frustrations, but about your unfulfilled potential. Concern yourself not with what you tried and failed in, but with what it is still possible for you to do.

—Pope John XXIII

Troubles can be frustrating, and how we view them is a test of character that could likewise be a stress inducer, if we permit it. Acknowledging our frustrations without dwelling on them is like looking at the wrong end of a telescope. Viewing our difficulties through one end of the glass magnifies them; turning it around reduces them to mere specks on our landscapes.

When faced with a problem or fear, we can choose to cling or fling. Imagine tossing our frustrations and replacing them with an attitude of hope. Now that we have put our problems in perspective, we can focus on our hopes and dreams. What possibilities would we like on our horizon? Let's make a list of our desires. Are we allowing anything to get in the way of these dreams? Many of our ambitions could become a reality and are within our realm of capabilities.

I will do something today from my list of dreams.

April 19

Enjoy the little things in life, for one day you may look
back and realize they were the big things.

—Antonio Smith

With light streaming through the arc of brilliant green trees, the sun
appears to pause briefly atop the tree canopy before it makes its rapid
descent. As I head off for a walk before dinner, I drink in all the visual
beauty of my surroundings. The scent of honeysuckle tickles my nose. A
neighbor dog barks hello to me, and I greet him in turn. Today it seemed
a flare up was edging in, but I didn't want to pass up an opportunity to
enjoy nature. Bursting with gratitude for the sights and smells present, I
arrive at a park and welcome the gentle breeze that greets me.

By enjoying the extraordinary beauty in God's ordinary creations, we
can appreciate the little things that help reshape a challenging day into
a lovely one, where our symptoms may not loom so ominous. Whether
walking in green spaces, playing with our young children, or enjoying a
hobby, we can carve out a bit of relaxation every day. Relishing the simple
things encourages contentment, even happiness, while boosting our moods
and physical well-being.

I will look for and find that small but wondrous element
that I might have missed in my life thus far.

April 20

The real art of conversation is not only to say the right thing at the right place but also to leave unsaid the wrong thing at the tempting moment.

—Dorothy Nevill

For some of us, the desire to communicate is one of our top emotional needs. Deprivation of this art form can even cause depression. Whether it is a lively chat shared with an old friend or a serious discussion of finances, there is skill involved in rendering the exchange a smooth one.

Not everyone possesses the talent of conversation. The ability to communicate with ease includes the balance of listening and speaking. Facial expressions, eye contact, and occasional head nods indicate we are attentive to the other person. Putting aside whatever we may be engaged in and giving full attention to the dialogue shows an interest. An excellent opportunity to practice communication is when we are sharing a meal with a friend. As we pause to savor our food, we can mull over words spoken, providing time to reflect on the content of the exchange before talking.

Another circumstance to put into practice the give-and-take of communication is a support group (especially before and after the meeting begins). We can make blunders in a known environment while practicing the skill of conversing.

I will continue practicing the art of conversation.

April 21

To eat is a necessity, but to eat intelligently is an art.
—Francois La Rochefoucauld

Many of us have food sensitivities or other symptoms that, along with irritable bowel syndrome, may leave our stomachs queasy on occasion (to say the least). These complications can narrow our food choices, and enjoying a meal in public might sometimes be challenging. Going out for a meal could become a troublesome and often-taxing chore of explaining what we can eat. Perhaps we are served the wrong food, and we either start over or get exasperated and depart.

When we are dining out with others, it can be helpful to discuss our limitations with the host or hostess before the event, and if we are going to a restaurant, choosing our selections by telephone in advance is an option. It may be easier to mention foods and condiments we *can* eat rather than spouting off a long list to our hostess of what we cannot. With a little planning on our part, mealtimes can turn into pleasurable experiences of eating well in a relaxed environment.

I will take into account
my food sensitivities when dining out.

April 22

A sponge has that much absorbent capability, and after a
while you can pour water over it and nothing stays.
—Itzhak Perlman

We may encounter intervals when simple activities can turn into
overwhelming and yes, depressing problems. If we are already including
walking in our day-to-day schedules, we may not realize walking on an
incline (such as a gentle slope) might cause us unforeseen difficulties.
Perhaps mending a garment is a possibility, but if we attempt to sew an
entire dress, our efforts may never come to fruition. After climbing a few
stairs, we may assume, "Yes, let's climb even more or hike over boulders!"
If we are unsuccessful, thinking plausibly that our bodies are failing us,
our emotions may give way to anger or depression.

Baby steps! Sometimes it is by way of small steps that we attain our
goals; we cannot force more upon our bodies when they are already at
our limit. By adjusting to this reality, we can adapt and cope with the
parameters of our physical limitations. Being thankful for the mobility
and accomplishments we enjoy can foster an upbeat and positive mood.
And together with the help of a physician and physical therapist, we may
achieve an increased level of activity.

By relishing my capabilities,
I will realize the reward of a sense of accomplishment.

April 23

Technical skill is mastery of complexity, while creativity is mastery of simplicity.

—Erik Christopher Zeeman

While sitting in my car at a small-town favorite drive-in restaurant, I notice a group of golden pansies dancing in the breeze. The flowers, with their little golden and dark faces, remind me of a family of yellow panda bears huddled together. A crow drops from the sky and the pansies/pandas halt as if sensing its presence. The bird rises with a start, and much to my amusement, the flowers resume their quake.

Oh, the joys of the simpler things humble me, ease my pain, and quiet my spirit as I once more offer up my prayer of thanks that I can enjoy the simple things.

There are numerous ways for us to tap into our creative side, whether through mental or physical activity. Merely engaging in original thought or action steers us on a more fundamental track, leaving the complexities—and the anxiety that comes with them—behind. We can explore our creative tendencies by searching for beauty in ordinary surroundings and becoming adept at acknowledging simple pleasures, wherever we may encounter them.

By tapping into my creative side today,
I will savor simplicity,

April 24

Shoot for the moon. Even if you miss, you'll land among
the stars.

—Les Brown

Attitudes have a way of brightening up when we are in pursuit of a goal,
no matter the degree of complexity. The challenges we pursue give rise
to a fuller, all-embracing life, one that allows for errors while continually
developing in wonder and awe.

Now when we decide on goals, let's not disqualify anything. If we
desire to attempt something, we should give it a go. Even secondary goals
can be rewarding, and trying them is part of the process and possible
fun. To incorporate more amusement in our day, we can try activities like
buying an inexpensive watercolor kit and splashing some paint on paper;
although it may not be a Rembrandt, we can relish the beauty of the colors
and the reward realized from creating colorful art.

Attempting demanding projects occasionally without focusing on the
outcome lends itself to total relaxation. We can learn to enjoy every stage
along the way, from approaching an objective to acquiring it, welcoming
ultimate enjoyment into our lives.

I will set forth a goal today,
even a tiny one.

April 25

Anxiety is the space between the "now" and the "then."
—Richard Abell

There is that moment in time—that suspension of ideas—when we have alternatives in how we judge an action. What distinguishes those of us with anxiety from others is the self-imposed panic we may feel to act *now,* a force to do something immediately.

Learning new approaches to our problems will often reveal that there is no urgency. Anxiety is often a learned response, and we can, with practice, replace it with healthier measures. By detaching mentally from the necessity to fix, speak, or defend, fight or flight sheds new light on where our anxiety originates. We may feel it comes from an outside source, although we create this uncomfortable feeling in our own minds.

A new method can be to introduce a pause when we are frustrated or pressured; this reduces anxiety and any need for present action. By pausing, we can bring more clarity to the situation and experience a calm and serene demeanor that we adopt as our own.

This moment can be as enjoyable as I make it.
Practicing healthy responses can help me to achieve comfort.

April 26

Physical activity can get you going when you are immobilized. Get action in your life, and don't just talk about it.

—John Davidson

Let's get outdoors and delight in a stroll through our neighborhoods or perhaps invest in a three-wheeled bicycle. The idea is to engage in physical activity daily. When we are able, we can try parking a little farther away from our destination. Or if we are in the mood for a walk while the weather is rainy, we might try visiting a store and grabbing a cart to hold onto and enjoy a leisurely outing in a climate-controlled atmosphere. No purchase is necessary. Let's only take pleasure in the walking. It is easier to walk faster without concern for balance or tripping while holding onto a cart, and bringing a container of water will keep us hydrated.

Most cities have various exercise classes that are appropriate for all levels of fitness. We can consider joining one that has a heated pool where we can discover the joy of being physical in warm water (a balm for sore muscles). We can purchase a training DVD (some are specific to our needs) or watch a televised workout program designed for our limits. Whatever type of fitness we select, pacing ourselves and having fun is the beneficial aim. By participating in positive self-help, such as exercise, we invest in a long-range goal in addition to enjoying immediate uplifting benefits.

I will begin exercising today.
It doesn't have to be fancy or expensive;
it just must get me moving.

April 27

If you let fear of consequence prevent you from following your deepest instinct, then your life will be safe, expedient and thin.

—Katherine Butler Hathaway

Following our deepest instincts feels natural, real, and distinctly our own. Although there could be consequences from following our *every* instinct, periodically the outcome can be affirmative and beneficial.

Life carries risk, and if we are to live abundant lives, an occasional risk will typically be involved. We can become dull by continually doing the familiar and following the obvious path. Let's attend a concert, learn to crochet, visit a museum or butterfly garden, ride a bike, learn to swim, or try that new restaurant. Trusting our instincts and making effective decisions while setting aside space in our schedules for fun and adventure is a recipe for wellness. Not letting fear prevent us from healthy new experiences enables individual growth and a more relaxed state where healing can commence.

I will not be afraid
to attempt something new.

April 28

Nothing that grieves us can be called little: by the eternal laws of proportion a child's loss of a doll and a king's loss of a crown are events of the same size.

—Mark Twain

Those of us who have been diagnosed with a chronic condition may all encounter losses at some point. It usually begins with physical abilities; later, our illness may disrupt, terminate, or cause friction in our relationships. By acknowledging our feelings, we accept these changes in our health for the loss that they are and the capacity they possess to touch our lives in often-profound ways.

Securing a moment to grieve for our loss of abilities while seeking improved means to move about and exercise can retain working muscles and prevent atrophy. It is conceivable, with effort and time, that we could regain most of our previous physical abilities.

We can gain perspective from any form of a loss by directing attention toward our positive activities and accomplishments. Because no one can judge how we feel, to refrain from minimizing our experiences, without magnifying them, can be constructive. Any loss is capable of inflicting damage; through treating ourselves with extra care during the interval, we provide ourselves with the love and support we deserve.

I will acknowledge any loss I sustain,
not comparing it to another's.

April 29

An education isn't how much you have committed to memory, or even how much you know. It's being able to differentiate between what you do know and what you don't.

—Anatole France

One of my favorite sayings has become, "I never know what I am going to forget." Another is, "If I remember something, I remember it … mostly." When my children were younger, they found it hilarious when I would say things like, "Go hang up your coats in the refrigerator." We enjoyed big belly laughs during those flubs. Fibro fog continues to yield some funny moments where I often discover humor in my occasional confusion.

When we are experiencing fibro fog, we may witness a reduction in our vocabulary, which can change from day to day, hour to hour, and even moment to moment. Instead of struggling with the uncertainty, let's appreciate that if today is not a day of clarity, tomorrow very well may be. By accepting our occasional glitches in memory and speech, we reduce frustrations. We unwittingly make many mistakes in the use of language. By viewing a share of our slips with a sense of humor, we can ease the adverse effects fibro fog may cause us.

I will accept the times when I experience fibro fog,
and I will be grateful for my moments of clarity.

April 30

Our entire life consists ultimately in accepting ourselves
as we are.

—Jean Anouilh

In a world that often worships beauty and places much emphasis on body shapes (in particular for women), it is not surprising that many of us develop self-esteem issues stemming from a skewed sense of body image. Additional health challenges, such as hypothyroidism, side effects of medication, and the inability to exercise strenuously, may initiate unintentional weight gain in some.

In our environment, an old fruit tree brandishing a gnarled bark and knots is deemed to be quite beautiful. But give us a few imperfections, and we wail. Why is it that when we see a less-than-beautiful animal, we think, *Oh, how cute.* However, with people, we might recoil from the dull or misshapen.

If we fail to recognize our beauty, a good habit is smiling into a mirror at least three times a day. Consider asking a good friend or family member what they like about us. This gives us the benefit of another's vision, and we may begin viewing ourselves with fresh eyes. Accepting ourselves with all our imperfections and beauty is paramount to commence healing.

I accept my whole beautiful self—my color,
shape, and size, with every scar and defect, acknowledged,
though not emphasized.

May 1

Just because you're miserable doesn't mean you can't enjoy your life.

—Annette Goodheart

Sure, we have chronic health issues, but that does not define our every waking thought and deed. Taking stock of our actions today, we can ask ourselves what constructive activities we pursue. A few examples of activities that can move us in the direction of a more functioning existence are: starting a project that brings us enjoyment; attending a support group and meeting like-minded people; taking an undemanding, fun class and perhaps asking a friend to join us; getting in touch with an old friend; visiting a neighborhood worship center; and doing a kind deed for someone anonymously.

Any pursuit that moves us in the direction of positive growth will suffice. Our aim? Enjoying life.

As I achieve new approaches to living,
enthusiastic feelings about myself surface.

May 2

Never grow a wishbone, daughter, where a backbone
ought to be.

—Clementine Paddleford

If wishing accomplished anything, we would probably be at the front of
the line, our trailing list in hand, with demands aplenty, waiting none too
patiently for our requests to be granted. We may succumb to a pattern of
wishing that everything in life were better, easier, and faster, and so on.
The daily demands of living with a chronic illness might foster this type
of reflection.

Some of us may be fortunate to have family members who understand
our chronic condition, discerning when to give us our independence and
when we need assistance—while treating us with respect and consideration
that all deserve. There will be occasions when asking for help—never easy
for the self-reliant—is in our best interest.

If there is no one to depend on, we may have to hire help when needed. By
keeping telephone numbers handy, including local pharmacies and grocers
that deliver, we cultivate organization and self-reliance. Independence may
feel healthiest, although occasional assistance (especially while in a flare
up) can help us rebound earlier and resume self-sufficient mode.

I will seek assistance when I am in need.

May 3

These are days when no one should rely unduly on his competence. Strength lies in improvisation. All the decisive blows are struck left-handed.

—Walter Benjamin

We make plans, like what to prepare for dinner or perhaps where to go out for the evening. Or it could be a daytime event. The reality is that our intentions often get quickly and painfully interrupted by symptoms of our condition. Here are some options:

- If we have a family and our children are of a responsible age, consider appointing the oldest head chef for a meal.
- Perhaps if we are lacking helpers, try rendering it a soup and sandwich affair, and light some candles for ambiance.
- Recline (with eyes shut) and breathe slow and easy for fifteen or twenty minutes.
- We can position our back or neck/shoulders on a heating pad in a comfortable chair and take a break for fifteen minutes or more. Then we may be able to resume our plans.

Even on the best of days, there will be times when inventiveness comes in handy. We can make a list of alternative ideas, and should a sudden onslaught of pain or any troublesome symptom occur at an inopportune moment, we are equipped with options.

I will begin improvising. It is merely coping creatively.

May 4

Life, an age to the miserable, and a moment to the happy.
—Francis Bacon

We may all, now and again, reach a disquieted point, a juncture when we feel that no one cares about us. We might experience grumpiness, whereby negative thinking and reacting could increase our myriad of symptoms and force reality to a slow crawl. Recognizing that feelings of self-pity may arise on occasion, we can choose to shift our thoughts toward the health-giving and affirmative.

Excessively thinking or talking about our health problems will drag us (and those around us) down mentally and physically. Imagine illness as two weighty suitcases. Suppose we were to carry them around all day. What an undesirable impact that would impose upon our dispositions. Let's put them down and lighten our load. Let's try to sprinkle positive and affirming thoughts throughout our day.

Reaching for opportunities that lift spirits can be an occasion to welcome happiness into our lives. Taking a shower, dressing in a flattering style, saying yes to an invitation, donning a smile, and appreciating what positive transformation small actions can generate in our day can all help to paint a brighter picture of our today.

I will be happy—and delight in the advantages it extends me.

May 5

Make your judgment trustworthy by trusting it.
—Greenville Kleiser

It's called second guessing for a reason. Instead of going with our first opinion or choice, we ponder another. Do we second guess ourselves? Are we frequently questioning if we are pursuing the right path concerning personal health or well-being? If we cease to believe in ourselves, self-doubt and unproductivity may transpire. Life's struggles can often rob us of natural abilities. Before our health capacity was diminished, we probably formulated decisions with greater ease.

Mistakes are part of everyone's reality. By possessing faith in ourselves, allowing that we all make errors and plowing on, we keep in the mix of things removing a sick stigma from our self-image. Whether the decisions we encounter are trivial or significant, beginning to trust our judgment can restore our confidence, and acting on our individual choices with assurance is the beginning of believing in our judgment.

I have trust and confidence in myself
and my decisions.

May 6

Notice that the stiffest tree is most easily cracked, while
the bamboo or willow survives by bending with the wind.
—Bruce Lee

We may observe that a mighty tree has minimal protection against the forces of nature. We may think a towering pine, for instance (so vast you cannot reach around it), surely must have the strength to withstand gale-force winds. Then we go out the day after a storm, and to our surprise, the tiniest of saplings remains standing after swaying and blowing about, surviving because of its elasticity, while there is damage to the huge pine.

Chronic illness is like a storm inflicting damage to our bodies and weakening our spirits with a constant barrage of symptoms. It is easy to feel like snapping under the weight of struggles with our health. We can benefit from discovering the workable approach to adapting.

By mimicking a willow moving with fluidity, remaining flexible and changing directions as necessary, we develop endurance through suppleness and resilience in the face of any chaos. This flexibility is useful in movement in addition to our dealings with everyday circumstances. We can appreciate that our worth is not only about physical strength but a compilation of our many character assets.

My flexibility in the face of countless adversities
will encourage my wellness.

May 7

Life is made up, not of great sacrifices or duties, but of little things, in which smiles, and kindnesses, and small obligations, given habitually, are what win and preserve the heart and secure comfort.

—Humphrey Davy

Opening our hearts to medically challenged people can be an occasion to give freely of ourselves. This lending compassion is so gratifying that it can regularly elevate our moods in the process. Helping a friend by lightening his or her load of pain and despair may seem unproductive for *our* health; however, quite the opposite, by being fully present for another, we are gifted in return.

One ingredient of giving to others is the ease of a warm smile, placed at the appropriate moment; there is nothing kinder. There may be instances when merely listening to another's story can be a selfless act of consideration. When we are not in a flare up, we may possess the energy to help others. Sharing our time with one in need reminds us of the benefits of reaching out beyond our world, listening, and extending a smile while offering a shoulder or a hug.

I will show kindness and caring
to someone with diminished health today.

May 8

If you follow your bliss, you put yourself on a kind of
track, which has been there all the while waiting for you,
and the life that you ought to be living is the one you are
living.

—Joseph Campbell

It's hard to maintain a positive direction when we are regularly accosted
with severe symptoms of our illness daily. Knowing when to put aside the
frustration and worry that comes with the unknown takes practice.

Let's begin the quest for what fulfills our happiness. Generally, these
actions bring a sense of well-being and serenity. Knowing we have our own
niche in life alleviates some of the hardships of having chronic medical
issues. Perhaps we are fortunate enough to be happily employed, or it could
be volunteer work, doing crafts, or antiquing. We can follow whatever
brings us joy. We all have something positive to focus on besides our
syndrome. Observation is our only requisite.

I encourage my healing and happiness
by seeking that which promotes my satisfaction and well-being.

May 9

Trust in God and do something.

—Mary Lyon

When approaching challenges, we may hear that praying is advantageous, although *we* must do the footwork. New paths may begin unfolding, through prayer, as we incorporate our ideas and actions. Some of our choices will encourage healing; others can help us cope with our lives in general.

By weighing our options and perhaps listing them, highlighting various choices, we can gain perspective on various routes to take. Then when we choose to postpone a major decision till another day, we allow an interval for reflection, which can enhance our clarity.

Prayer is a helpful tool that offers the capability to move beyond a situation or uncomfortable place in our lives through the guidance we obtain. A portion of our struggles will require action or decisions; others, we will have to let go. So often that which appears overwhelming at night can become more manageable in the light of day. As we welcome God's guidance, we discover comfort in the unburdening and a strategy for the footwork.

I will trust God as my guide.

May 10

As long as you keep a person down, some part of you has to be down there to hold him down, so it means you cannot soar as you otherwise might.
—Marian Anderson

Spending any effort attempting to control another person can weaken us ultimately, as to control or be controlled is not a healthy state. It is more conducive to our well-being to concentrate on the positive attributes of both ourselves and others. If we have the power to do good for another person, this can enable us to attain new heights emotionally.

A few weaknesses are an unavoidable part of everyone's makeup. Our responsibility is to detect our strengths and any flaws and work on them, leaving others to do their individual housecleaning. Let's look for ways to focus on our assets, thus enhancing our self-esteem.

I will cease any attempt to control another person,
thereby using my energy
to expand my own wings.

May 11

Minds are like parachutes—they only function when open.

—Lord Thomas Dewar

It is through the constant stretching of our margins that growth continues and learning capabilities expand. The following are a few activities that we can apply to maintain active minds: read an informative and thought-provoking book, have a lively discussion on a current topic, tackle a difficult crossword puzzle, or indulge in a game that involves memory, math, or both—such as backgammon.

The problems we face can inspire us to keep our intellects open, thus furthering knowledge. We can use the multitude of resources available to research our health challenges, and discovering documented pharmaceutical or nutritional support to assist with our slurry of symptoms will help us maintain alert and confident minds. By endeavoring toward what was once believed to be unattainable, we can aspire to new heights, accomplishing fresh approaches to old ideas. Our abilities are limitless.

I can launch thoughts of extensive capabilities in my mind.

May 12

I've learned to take time for myself and to treat myself
with a great deal of love and a great deal of respect 'cause
I like me ... I think I'm kind of cool.

—Whoopi Goldberg

At times we may judge ourselves harshly, pressuring our already complicated lifestyles. For the most part, fibromyalgia patients are type A personalities (driven, high achievers) before diagnosis. One of the characteristics is being a control freak or a perfectionist. Sound familiar? Or maybe not. Perhaps we are one of the laid-back type B personalities.

Post-diagnosis can be an opportunity for new experiences and discoveries about us, smoothing the way for us to accept ourselves as human beings with all our glorious and inglorious successes and failures. Let's practice smiling at our image in a mirror and treating ourselves as well as we treat other people. This can be our foundation of self-love.

Now is the time to do something I enjoy
that makes me smile
and feel good about me.

May 13

The best remedy for a short temper is a long walk.
—Joseph Joubert

Walking away from a situation that has accelerated into anger on anyone's part is a wise move. Should anger surface, exercise (walking particularly) offers distance and perspective from any problem and is a safe way to calm tempers that can escalate on occasion. Initially, there may be a tendency to revisit the hurt through our thoughts, and there could be tears of frustration. After a few minutes of plodding along, we may notice our pace has slowed, and a flower, butterfly, or gecko have riveted our attention with a smooth heartbeat and a tranquil mood.

When our feelings are ablaze, we can begin the process of emotional healing by rectifying any wrongdoing and asking for forgiveness if necessary. When our temper does escalate, we can apply appropriate and acceptable anger. Later, when we are calm, we can attempt to identify if we have overreacted and how better to deal with it in the future, putting us on a path to better emotional health. Recognizing anger as an emotion keeps it in perspective and lessens its impact, making way for peace to resurface.

I gain a measure of control
when I walk my anger away.

May 14

Be not afraid of life. Believe that life is worth living, and
your belief will help create the fact.

— Henry James

Life, for some with chronic medical problems, may hardly be endurable.
If we have slipped into this limited way of thinking, we might have
misplaced our belief system in the simple goodness of life. Let's remember
the direction in the story of Peter Pan that if we believe, we must clap our
hands. A childlike acceptance and wonder can be a healing technique for
those who are health compromised.

We can exhibit gratitude for uplifting beliefs and the renewed sense
of happiness that we experience in our lives. Believing that life is worth
living requires hope that can light the way through the dark alleyways of
our lifetime. While living, loving, and clapping, we may find that fear has
taken a backseat in our lifeboat named *Believe*.

I believe my existence has value
and I have hope.

May 15

It was impossible to get a conversation going. Everybody was talking too much.

—Yogi Berra

I grew up in New Orleans. You can't get more Southern than that! I noticed in my travels that I could start up a conversation in the South with a stranger, but it is more of an art and challenge for me away from home. I found that sometimes knowing when not to speak was just as important as talking.

Chronic illnesses can frequently leave us feeling isolated from people; however, at times, a sincere desire to communicate can arise. Listening and communication are skills worth learning and practicing. They keep us connected to others and dispel isolation.

Our desire to know another person, from light conversation to in-depth sharing, enables us to hone our skills when we are able. We may hear that we never learn anything while we are talking. Who knows—there might be a reward of wit and wisdom springing forth from individuals of various ranks and ages. We can give ourselves a cheer of encouragement for each time we put our woes aside and listen to another's views and feelings.

I will engage in the art of conversation today.

May 16

Maturity is the ability to think, speak and act your feelings within the bounds of dignity. The measure of your maturity is how spiritual you become during the midst of your frustration.

—Samuel Ullman

How do we, as adults, tackle frustrations? Are we quick to form opinions that may contain harsh criticisms of ourselves or others? Perhaps in our pain and irritation, our actions are less than stellar. It may be tempting to lean on others for direction, comfort, and guidance, or perchance we opt to go it alone in an often-clumsy attempt to handle the complexities of our ever-shifting health challenges.

During the many episodes of distress along our journey, the addition of a spiritual foundation to call upon is a godsend. Our Creator can replace that bundle of raw feelings with, "Relax—I've got this," thus leaving our emotions calmer, more centered. By turning over frustrations to Him, we heighten spirituality and liberation from unnecessary tension. Releasing troubles in this way is a gratifying means of coping with life's annoyances.

I can take a mature direction to my burdens today
by adopting a spiritual approach.

May 17

Let not your heart be troubled, neither let it be afraid.
—John 14:27

With the presence of so many unknown factors surrounding our condition, we may find ourselves faced with many decisions concerning well-being and fitness. The debate continues as to what causes our chronic illness, and this may produce fear in some because of the unknown element. There may be a foundation for a few of our fears, while others are simply worrying on overdrive.

Questioning whether any concerns have a base of probable or presumed outcomes can help diminish speculative fear. If we find we are fixating on a decision and turning it into a worry instead of using sound reasoning, we can stop and take a break. We could go for a walk, watch a tranquil movie, or use an alternative form of peaceful diversion to unclutter our hearts and heads until we know how to approach from an encouraging perceptive. Participating in confidence-boosting activities can result in the shedding of many an old fear.

I will not let fear control me.

May 18

I like work: it fascinates me. I can sit and look at it for hours.

—Jerome K. Jerome

When our energy falters, we may want to do nothing more than pull the covers over our heads and drift into a state of resignation when even the *thought* of work tasks cause us to be overwhelmed. We could become dazed just thinking of everything that requires doing, and once again, the strength and motivation necessary to begin our day may be lacking.

Aiming somewhere in between that state and endeavoring to maintain some element of work every day can provide a compelling sense of achievement. Even the simplest of chores, like organizing the clutter on our desk, hanging up our clothes, or making our beds, can boost our spirits with a feeling of accomplishment.

Prioritizing can determine whether a task or event gets completed or attended, dismissed, or delayed. The satisfaction of completing even the most mundane of tasks can put a smile on our faces, bringing about a job-well-done outlook.

Today I will recognize a work project that gives me satisfaction, and I will relish the outcome.

May 19

Any concern too small to be turned into a prayer is too
small to be made into a burden.

—Corrie ten Boom

Oh, the worries and concerns we have. Will there ever be a treatment for
fibromyalgia that alleviates all our symptoms? How long will I continue
to feel this way? Where did I put my glasses, my keys? Worries come in all
shapes and sizes, and those of us who have a chronic medical condition
could have an abundance.

Have we tried prayer? Just humbly daily praying, nothing angry or
bargaining. When we go about our daily routine, we might sometimes
neglect prayer. Perhaps the key for those with health issues is to pray often.
This can help keep our difficulties from mushrooming, thereby shrinking
them to a manageable size. Some of our finest praying is when we simply
talk to God and listen to His guidance.

There are undeniably too many things about which to worry. Without
prayer, we take on problems that are not meant for our shoulders. When
we persistently lean on God, letting Him handle the small and the big, it
lightens our load and leaves us with grateful, relaxed attitudes.

Prayer allows my body and mind
to function on a healthier level.

May 20

Hope is the thing with feathers
That perches in the soul,
And sings the tune without the words,
And never stops at all ...

—Emily Dickinson

After our diagnosis, we may face days when life seems just not worth the trouble. Stress and anxiety affect us more than the average individual, and living with a chronic condition may cause numerous shifts in relationships. We may experience abundant trials because of debilitating symptoms and might feel alone, and hope may seem to be only an elusive word. Chaos disguised as fibro fog may dwell in our midst. This is when the need to listen to our calm inner voice (or song) is greatest.

It takes a bit of relaxation to heed our inner song. Stripping away stress and tension and laying bare our soul's inner strength may be the help and healing balm that we need. Before we realize it, we have found our way back from despair to hope. Hope can be a constant presence that enlightens our very souls. Embracing that newfound hope can guide us gently through our life ventures.

I will listen to my soul's song: "Hope."

May 21

A real friend is one who walks in when the rest of the
world walks out.

—Walter Winchell

For those with chronic health issues, friendship can sometimes be
problematic. Complications from our symptoms often get in the way of
impromptu get-togethers and rob us of our energy with little warning.
Pushing past these limitations to maintain friendships is truly worth the
effort.

Knowing we have a friend or friends who look past our struggles and
can see the person instead of just the illness can help form lasting bonds.
Our shared laughter and tears are just a part of what forge enduring
friendships.

While *our* hurdle is a chronic condition, our healthier friends may have
their own set of woes. Facing our troubles together, setting forth hand in
hand, is the essence of friendship.

I am thankful for friends who truly like me.

May 22

The most effective way to cope with change is to help create it.

—L. W. Lynett

Change is scary. How do we know an alternative will be superior to the familiar? We don't, although there is always room for growth and we won't know until we try. Coping with change is one facet of learning to deal with our syndrome. Now and again, we may appear to be helpless to the many changes that are occurring. Here are some suggestions to help lessen the limitations that can happen with chronic illness:

- We can accept that there will be adjustments and adaptations in our lives to fit our new requirements and abilities.
- If asked, we can help our families to understand our condition.
- Let's not overdo it but having a moderate exercise routine (including stretching) that is explicitly formulated for fibromyalgia.

Being unafraid to initiate change can be one of the more challenging hurdles. It may be easier to fall back into complacency. As we begin to modify previous options with a determined attitude, the results can be gratifying.

I will create some change in my life today,
even if it is a small one.

May 23

Celebrate the happiness that friends are always giving.
Make every day a holiday and celebrate just living!
—Amanda Bradley

Becoming bogged down in the intricacies of chronic illness to the extent of pushing pleasurable people and events aside is something we should resist. We might be too hasty, finding a flaw in every plan or a reason to decline every invitation. If we fall into this pattern, it can lead to alienating our support systems (valuable friendships providing emotional encouragement and physical assistance) and possibly distancing any new friends.

Having family members or friends give of their time with caring gestures is worthy of celebrating. We can revel in the simple joy of being alive! Wouldn't it be a delight to seize the day and celebrate? Experiencing health challenges doesn't mean we can't gather with and enjoy the company of others. When we are joined together with happy people, any day can be like a holiday.

Live. Love. Laugh.

May 24

The line between failure and success is so fine … that we are often on the line and do not know it.

—Elbert Hubbard

The endless battle we face of chronic medical issues could cause some of us to back away from formulating goals, although others may be in pursuit of the latest research and the desire for success about our condition. From our choice of a knowledgeable healthcare team to everyday matters, we could ask ourselves, "Am I considering my situation and my options from all perspectives?" By exploring both the pros and cons of circumstances and establishing clear objectives before formulating choices, we can prevent failure from becoming the norm. Obtaining goals can be more realistic if we relieve some of the pressure and refrain from strict, self-imposed schedules.

We might consider whether anxiety may be influencing any of our actions. Whether we are experiencing apprehensive of success or failure, releasing a portion of our struggles through prayer and meditation can be beneficial. Nonetheless, we gradually advance toward wellness, maintaining our goals and celebrating achievements as we encounter them, while bolstering our self-esteem.

I can facilitate my chances of success
by reflecting on what motivates my choices.

May 25

Feelings are much like waves—we can't stop them from coming but we can choose which one to surf.

—Jonatan Martensson

Some of our mood shifts may stem from hormonal changes, side effects of medication, chemical imbalances, or food allergies, to name a few. Any of these may have us out of sorts on occasions. These changes are easier to accept when we recognize they are fleeting. Occasionally our friends and families may not comprehend that our condition affects our moods. Taking a breather is deemed best if we are in a bit of a mood. We can try spending a few minutes rejuvenating alone and later connect with others when we feel better.

An uplifting, fun way to connect and pass the time amicably while we are moody is to play a game that allows laughter and happy noise. Any game that encourages acting out fun scenarios, drawing, or singing also allows the release of pent-up feelings. Emotions can beneficially bubble to the surface, and everyone who is participating will profit while having fun.

I will reach for a game (or a time-out)
when my moods overwhelm me.

May 26

Hey, ho! There's more to life than cheekbones.

—Kate Winslet

We can accept our God-given beauty and with a little effort, keep up our appearance without it turning into a hassle. Those of us with health issues may struggle to maintain a fit body, but to be fresh and neat isn't that complicated. Daily maintenance without stressing about our looks is mood elevating. Showering or bathing, running a comb through our hair, and putting on a touch of lip gloss can enhance our image and outlook daily.

Even on the worst days, we can put on a smile, that most essential ingredient of our physical bodies. Smiling feels delightful! Stretching those face muscles attempts nothing other than a lifted spirit. The results are amazing, both for ourselves and for those with whom we interact. Concentrating on the finer qualities and overlooking minor flaws teases propitious smiles to the surface.

Smile for the endorphins, and reap the rewards.

May 27

Draw a crazy picture, Write a nutty poem,
Sing a mumble-grumble song,
Whistle through your comb.
Do a loony-goony dance "Cross the kitchen floor ..."
—Shel Silverstein

Today while I was in the grocery store, I came upon a grandmother pushing her grandbaby in the grocery cart. The piped-in music had a good beat, and we were both swaying slightly to the music. We shared a smile and hello as our carts passed, our day a bit brighter. My favorite spontaneous activity is to break into dance. Admittedly, depending on my energy level, this dance may sometimes last only a few seconds, or sometimes I can only manage to sway. I have noticed I feel healthiest and naturally happiest when I am able to be silly or engage in a bit of folly every day.

When we are battling an often-challenging condition, we can lessen its hold on us by engaging in lighthearted activities now and then. To aim for one every day would be excellent. We can loosen up and dare to have fun. Let's draw a lighthearted picture for our eyes only. There is no pressure to make it correct. Simply engage in the joy of drawing. Or we can sing or hum to a catchy tune on the radio, a music score on a television commercial, or perhaps give voice to a made-up ditty. Throwing caution to the wind, we can dance (or shuffle about) with a smile on our faces. Our burdens lift as we give ourselves the gift of a carefree, enlivening respite from a not-so-fun illness.

I will let loose and have fun
by not allowing my limitations
to mar my spontaneity.

May 28

The very least you can do in your life is to figure out what you hope for. And the most you can do is live inside that hope.

—Barbara Kingsolver

We can shore up our sense of achievement and confidence through assembling two lists consisting of our hopes. On the first let's include all that we have ever hoped for even though we may have uncertainties due to illness, finances, or perhaps age. Our second listing is a more practical approach. It is a record of the achievable. Somewhere between the two is our aim, and by merging both into a third, we stretch our possibilities.

Working from our options list and maintaining an enthusiastic attitude throughout the activity can be enlightening, precipitating a move toward progress. Our achievements perhaps could be true callings or talents that we have not tapped. As hope becomes a reality through our accomplishments, doubts recede, and we can begin to witness a shift in our moods to positive and uplifting. Latching onto any triumphs and claiming them as our own can help minimize stress and immune system fluctuations.

By making hope my daily companion,
my spirits rise, and I am at ease with living.

May 29

I've lived a life that's full,
I've traveled each and ev'ry highway,
And more, much more than this,
I did it my way.

—Paul Anka

How much control have we over our lives today? Are we doing things our way? Before health problems changed our lives, our norm might have been traveling the globe, being a busy mom, or enjoying productive work outside the home. We possibly have welcomed days filled with events and meaningful work. Did everything come to a grounding halt? What will we change in our lives now that they include a chronic illness diagnosis? If not for our deteriorating health issues, what would we carry out differently?

Many changes can be applied to enhance our health and relationships, providing a heightened sense of wellness. We can feasibly begin by gathering an inventory of desired changes concerning our lives and an inkling of how to accomplish these adjustments. Allowing for a flexible deadline will give us something to aim for, while we steadily improve our outlooks and continue to live life fully.

I will do at least one small thing today
my way.

May 30

I have come to realize that all my trouble with living has
come from fear …
> —Angela L. Wozniak

We may be attempting to shoulder the troubles of the world: disturbing
news of war, political unrest, famine, murder, domestic abuse, and worse.
When we do this, we are inviting anxiety and an amplified unease into our
existence. We can list our fears and rate their importance. Let's separate
them into categories of medically related, relationship, and general, thus
facilitating a further realization of where the significant portion of any fears
stem from. If we are worried about the various fibromyalgia complications,
this can increase tension and intensify our symptoms even further.

Letting go of that which we cannot control and bringing focus to
positive change in our already complicated lives can be something to attain.
As we adjust our daily living within the scope of our new limitations, there
can be a reduction in anxieties. Fear is an emotion, but let it not be the *one*
feeling that guides our actions.

I will replace my fears with courage—
courage in my life and all that I am.

May 31

If I have ever made any valuable discoveries, it has been
owing more to patient attention than to any other talent.
—Isaac Newton

While meandering on a picturesque path beside a small lake with sunlight
winking off the water, my attention was directed first to the stillness. I
then observed a little doe in the piney woods. She froze, watching me
approach for a minute, and then bounded over a slight hill. My attention
was quickly directed to the unmistaken honking of two Canadian geese.
I watched them glide over the lake surface and listened to their calls,
imagining the lead goose was insisting it knew the way and the other was
backseat driving. This scene unfolding made me chuckle to myself. When
I visit God's wondrous earth, a bounty of pleasures is always my reward.

What can we ascertain through the patient attention of our lives and
our place in it? We could keep a journal of discoveries to be visited at will,
having the ability to soothe our frazzled selves. Perhaps we have a flair
for effortlessly noticing the treasure of nature's delights. Maybe a short
walk alone in quiet without the chatter of everyday problems can reveal
something wondrous, such as a descending sun painted in lemon yellow
with touches of orange and magenta. At times we can share these treats of
sight and sound, other times we might hold some in reserve, bringing them
to awareness when their soothing properties are most needed.

The gift of nature can help create patience
and appreciation in me.

June 1

If one asks for success and prepares for failure, he will get
the situation he has prepared for.
—Florence Scovel Shinn

Compared to our more fit acquaintances, those of us with persistent
medical problems may commonly aim lower in our endeavors. We may
have been disappointed by many wrong turns on our journeys toward
wellness. The reality of our often-debilitating condition can be cause for
the intrusion of negative thoughts. Some may take to their beds and lose
hope. Let's rise and prepare for success by not giving up on ourselves and
seizing the opportunity for feats of accomplishments in our lives.

We can endeavor to view our health challenges with an optimistic
approach. Try this exercise. On a piece of paper write, "I am on a path
to good health." Now let's position this affirmation in a visible place,
repeating the statement aloud three times each day. Believing we can
succeed sends a healing message to the body, which in turn assists the
balance of our immune systems, which is so necessary for improved health.

I have faith in my successes.

June 2

As for relaxing, you can do it anywhere. It's merely a frame
of mind.

—Donatella Versace

When the pace of the world around us refuses to ease up, let's try slowing
down to maintain a calmer attitude by mentally detaching ourselves from
hectic situations. How profitable for our chronic condition to be able
to maintain a mellow healing disposition, regardless of a multitude of
stressful circumstances.

By the application of a calming, relaxed breathing technique, we can
put a damper on any nerve-racking situations. Through slow, practiced
breathing, our lungs and muscles receive more oxygen, which means an
increase in healthy energy and a more tranquil mood. If we catch ourselves
in worrisome thinking, we can replace it with encouraging ideas. We
can practice the twofold assistance of measured breathing and positive
thinking anywhere. The implementation is especially beneficial when we
are stuck in trying traffic jams. Our thoughts can remain peaceful when
we apply relaxing methods as a means of coping.

I can release my hold on troubling thoughts
and grasp those of tranquility instead.

June 3

The last moments (before a trip) are earthquake and convulsion, and the feeling that you are a snail being pulled off your rock.

—Anne Morrow Lindbergh

Travel may be draining and hectic, but through simple planning and time management, we can reduce or eliminate anxiety while traveling. If we pack as light as is feasible and toss a small blanket and pillow along with some reading material into a comfortable carry-on, our journeys can become more pleasurable. Unfortunately, delays are frequently part of travel, and if faced with delays, we can pass the time through people watching, an entertaining diversion. By engaging in a game of imagining where passersby are going and what their occupation may be, we create a fun way to idle away air travel time.

Alerting travel authorities should we need an assistive device prevents tears of exhaustion and pain if we later realize we require assistance and none is available. If we are touring alone, it might also be necessary to request assistance when lifting our luggage, freeing our energy for the journey. The process of planning for our comfort can move travel into a possibility. Then while we are discovering the joys of visiting favorite sights or enjoying new surroundings, any limitation is minimized as we expand our vistas.

I will leave behind my familiar setting for
the chance to experience new adventures.

June 4

Don't knock the weather; nine-tenths of the people couldn't
start a conversation if it didn't change occasionally.
—Kin Hubbard

We all experience superlative days when we are gifted with a startling
blue sky wrapped around bright green trees with a riot of colorful flowers.
However, there undoubtedly are other weather patterns that may not be
as welcomed. Sometimes just knowing adverse weather is heading in our
direction and thinking of the pain it triggers can inadvertently increase
our discomfort.

Rainstorms provoke a feeling of depression in some, bringing to light
how much our environment can influence our overall welfare. When
bodily pain accompanies these low-pressure barometric systems, we can
acknowledge this might alter our plans for the day. It could become an
opportunity to read a good book or organize our recipes. We can keep
easy-to-prepare foods on hand for just such happenings. By acknowledging
the local forecasts now and then but not making them the focus of our
attention, we help our pain levels remain in a more manageable range.

I will look upon the weather as an accompaniment to my day,
giving it recognition when necessary but without stressing over it.

June 5

By three methods we may learn wisdom: First by reflection, which is noblest; second, by imitation, which is easiest; and third by experience, which is the bitterest.

—Confucius

Now that we have fibromyalgia, it seems a new method of learning has become necessary to retain instructions or absorb printed material. We may discern it is often a laborious process as we approach gathering information in an unfamiliar way that can become bittersweet with our struggles due to cognitive symptoms. We may feel we are anything but wise.

Our struggles can lay down the foundation for experience and wisdom that we were unprepared though pleased to develop. Our challenge to work more efficiently during difficult intervals can bring its own type of wisdom—that of experience.

I will acknowledge my limitations when learning, lifting any anxiety.

June 6

If you are seeking creative ideas, go out walking. Angels whisper to a man when he goes for a walk.
—Raymond Inmon

Perhaps because of relentless fatigue or another symptom, we may have been less than active heretofore. When we learn that our pain and fatigue can improve with movement, we can seek a gradual change from being inactive to a modest degree of gentle exercise.

Light exercise is helpful. Why don't we start with a gentle walk surrounded by God's natural world? Nature is a known healer. Starting slow and gradually increasing intervals outdoors while making use of our muscles can initially feel laborious, but eventually it can develop into a pleasure. During a taxing day, if we are very fatigued, our stroll can be leisurely and brief, or if we are unable to walk sitting in the shade, breathing in the fresh air and welcoming the sights and sounds is a peaceful alternative. Let's try to leave telephones, music, electronic devices, or reading material behind as we open ourselves up to the calming healing properties of nature.

Today I will walk without destination or purpose;
I will walk simply for happiness and absolute pleasure.

June 7

In Rome you long for the country. In the country, you praise to the skies the distant town.

—Horace

Having medical issues occasionally generates a desire to trade in our bodies for a more healthful version—perhaps more often than we would like. We can fall into the trap of longing for what we lack (a permanent relief for what ails us is one) or what is conceived to be superior and devoid of problems. Persistent negative thinking becomes a weight that intensifies tension and disrupts our already challenged immune systems.

As an alternative, let's focus on the encouraging and enjoyable aspects of our setting, which promotes healthier living. We can seek out the pleasant in our lives, such as a park to meander in, a shaded bench on which to sit, or perhaps a local tranquil tea room or bookstore to frequent. By practicing acceptance and seeking the upbeat, we nourish our well-being while enriching our enjoyment.

Today I will focus on what I enjoy in every situation I encounter.

June 8

I keep the telephone of my mind open to peace, harmony, health, love, and abundance. Then, whenever doubt, anxiety, or fear try to call me, they keep getting a busy signal—and soon they'll forget my number.

—Edith Armstrong

Anxiety is one of the symptoms of our chronic condition. Some of us may experience anxiety more frequently than others, although we can lessen its impact on our fitness and well-being by our reaction. One way to reduce those anxious feelings is to try a gentle breathing exercise that can enable solace, thereby ushering in a sense of relaxation.

Let's start by standing with our feet aligned and shoulders relaxed, with our arms dangling at our sides. If we are unable to stand, we can sit in a firm chair with our hands upturned on our thighs. Next, soften the face and jaw and then add slow, deep breathing. As we begin breathing in through the nose to the count of four and exhaling slowly through the mouth for a count of eight, we create an in-the-moment sensation that can free up knotted muscles.

Experiment with introducing the words *peace* and *harmony* into our minds as we inhale and on the exhale saying and dispelling worry or doubt. This makes the exercise more effective. We can use words with personal meaning. Try using calming ones on the inhale and those we want to be free of on the exhale.

If I am encountering any anxiety today,
I will welcome peaceful relief by engaging
in a beneficial breathing exercise.

June 9

Dreams are illustrations ... from the book your soul is
writing about you.

—Marsha Norman

Have we ever woken from a vivid, well-scripted dream where it seemed we
were a character in a complex film? To flourish in better-quality sleep with
the bonus of recall of spectacular dreams could be an excellent change in
our nocturnal patterns.

Let's try making notes of our nighttime dream experiences. This
practice encourages right-brain creative thought. Dreaming can often
provide something beautiful to cleave to regardless of present circumstances,
although it is also a means of exposing any anxiety or fear and can include
troubling or disturbing nightmares where subconscious thoughts emerge.

Science does not agree on why we dream, but one theory is that it helps
us deal with stressful happenings in a healthy, safe manner and facilitates
memory and problem-solving. Studies show that in sleep, adults experience
approximately 20 percent in REM per night—dreaming. This part of the
cycle is essential to learning. While many may recall their dreams, others
rarely can. Certain medications, as well as advanced age, can interfere
with REM cycles. Through apportioning adequate slumber nightly, we
encourage dream phases and improved sleep with the bonus of memory
advantages.

Tonight I will sleep and perchance retain a peaceful dream,
instilling a sense of serenity.

June 10

Do just once what others say you can't do, and you will
never pay attention to their limitations again.
                                        —James R. Cook

Life with chronic medical problems establishes various limitations. We
might notice our activity level before a diagnosis is a thing of the past. When
we recognize and live within different limits, we may create boundaries
where none previously existed. By forming the decision about whether to
attend a gentle exercise class, take part in a local theater production, or
climb a flight of stairs, we establish our own limits.

There may be a trial-and-error phase that we confront, seizing what
we can accomplish without bringing on a flare up. By setting the pace, we
can augment our perception of who we are. As our restrictions are assessed
with some degree of caution, gradually adding new activities when feeling
capable, we promote a positive self-image.

I define my own abilities and limitations.

June 11

Hope, like the gleaming taper's light,
Adorns and cheers our way;
And still, as darker grows the night,
Emits a brighter ray.

—Oliver Goldsmith

Hope can be a slippery word for those of us with fibromyalgia. We may repeatedly hear or read there is no 100 percent fix for our chronic condition. It requires a certain effort to look past these pronouncements of despair and assume control of our own happiness.

Learning all we can about fibromyalgia enlightens us and reveals many options available for treatment. Keeping hope alive demands courage and strength. Although, even in the event of flare ups and setbacks, we can strive toward a useful approach with cheerful confidence. As we maintain our belief that happiness is possible, obtainable, even in the event of the darkness that can be chronic illness, we begin to visualize better health in our future. When we are seeking possibilities where gloom resides, hope can be our beacon of light.

I will own my happiness.

June 12

Do not fear mistakes—there are none.

—Miles Davis

Confusion. It figures prominently in our list of unwanted symptoms. One area of confusion many of us may find problematic is working with numbers. Whether it is our finances, giving or receiving change after a purchase, or figuring percentage for gratuities, we may repeatedly be incorrect in our calculations. Even using calculators may stump us now and again. Accepting that fibro fog is the culprit can take some of the sting out of repeated blunders.

We could find ourselves anxious because of our mistakes when we are dealing with people, money, or numbers, such as addresses, phone numbers, or zip codes. An old and familiar game of Monopoly can massage those memory cells that enable us to handle money. We can play Phase 10, Solitaire, or other games involving numbers or counting, helping to get over our tendency toward embarrassment while gaining confidence with the added benefit of fun. Our goal is that at the end of the day, we will not fear the occasional error, only casually note it.

I will approach mistakes with composure,
realizing they are part of everyone's experience.

June 13

If all flowers wanted to be roses, nature would lose her springtime beauty, and the fields would no longer be decked out with little wildflowers.

—Therese of Lisieux

In creating the vast diversity in life, God afforded us incredible gifts. Wouldn't it be dull if people were entirely alike, as well as everything in the natural world? We are a group of diverse people with a wide array of skills. While we may seem to be a simple wildflower compared to some, we might recollect that some of the rarest of treasures are the amazing flowers we call wild.

By recognizing our self-worth—our real inner beauty—we manage the emotional as well as physical effects of our health complications. Through discovering something to praise in ourselves every day, we mold our self-esteem and confidence. If we are unsure of our distinctive qualities, we can ask a trusted friend or family member to help identify our distinctiveness. This could be anything from perhaps a quirky cowlick to an ability to put others at ease, and they make up the special beings we are.

I acknowledge the extraordinary person I am.

June 14

Don't mind criticism. If it is untrue, disregard it, if it is unfair, keep from irritation, if it is ignorant, smile; if it is justified, learn from it.

—Author unknown

Those of us with fibromyalgia may sometimes hear, "How come you are the only one who_____"? Fill in the blank.

Everything from our food requirements, various sensitivities, and necessity for comfortable clothing and bedding may vary widely from the norm. On occasion, criticisms may come from people pointing out our many errors due to fibro fog.

Encountering negative comments and criticism can be challenging. It might be difficult to smile or ignore them when we want to cry or get irritated instead. We can take what we want from the unwanted advice and toss the rest. Keeping a calm head in the face of invalid assumptions will help put things back on track for the uplifting and encouraging.

I will not overreact to criticism.

June 15

Cherish forever what makes you unique, 'cuz you're really
a yawn if it goes!

—Bette Midler

Within each of us are unique characteristics that set us apart from others.
If we have traits such as a genuine, caring, and loving disposition, try
spreading it around. We might find it is contagious.

Perhaps a good sense of humor and an infectious laugh define our
personality. Laughter is encouraged, for it can release constricted muscles
and soften any frown lines. We can explore opportunities to share a joke
or listen to an amusing tale, creating intervals for unwinding and sharing
all that is light and upbeat.

Whether our talents are hidden or easily recognized, acknowledging
and embracing our gems fosters a well-rounded personality. If we are
searching for a self-esteem enhancement, we can write our merits in a
journal or in a location where we can evoke our uniqueness.

I will accept my uniqueness and appreciate my individuality.

June 16

He did it with all his heart, and prospered.

—2 Chronicles 31:21

It is not uncommon to search for new ways to improve our existence, as some previous approaches may no longer suffice. Along with news of our medical condition, stress can ramp up. At this juncture, it is often hard not to give way to depression and self-pity. As we encounter the multitude of adjustments in store for those with chronic medical issues, we may be in danger of losing hope, and doubt of any healing modifications may creep into our hearts.

Change is possible. We can make a list of what we *can* alter—such as healthier food choices or walking outdoors several times a week. Our list will give us something to aim for while inhibiting low moods, stress, and self-pity from taking root. Putting our whole hearts into any endeavor can garner satisfying results. To thrive even though we confront many health concerns can be a welcome gift, with change and effort—a beginning.

I will succeed in a hopeful future
by putting my heart into my efforts.

June 17

Because when we love, we always strive to become better
than we are.

—Paulo Coelho

Love is the ultimate gift, one that we can give and receive. Whether for a
family member, a friend, or a pet, this sheer emotion has been proven to
be healing by increasing our serotonin levels and enriching lives. Infants
deprived of love do not thrive; adults often seem to blossom when they
are in love.

The world is full of things to cherish. Perhaps we may have recently
dissolved a relationship, and a cooling-off period before easing back into
a commitment could be of benefit. If we are out of practice in this type
of association, we could start with houseplants. Caring for them prepares
us for the balance necessary in a healthy relationship. Too much water
(attention) is just as damaging as too little.

If we look to pets as our source of affection, our bonus is an abundance
of adoration. By adopting a canine or a feline friend, we feel a comforting
reward while snuggling with our pet. While we learn to embrace love, let's
not forget to put ourselves at the top of the list. Allowing this emotion to
shine within our actions and words can become something to which to
aspire.

I will experience the healing gift of love.

June 18

Don't get me wrong, I admire elegance and have an appreciation of the finer things in life. But to me, beauty lies in simplicity.

—Mark Hyman

Gazing around our homes for clutter will give us a bearing on where to begin to simplify. Let's start with donating any clothing items that we have not worn in a year or two. Doing the same with knickknacks that tend to accumulate over the years will eliminate hours spent cleaning. Downsizing our accumulated possessions can be the beginning of a life with a portion of the strain extracted.

It may become a liberating experience to rid ourselves of unnecessary trappings. Clutter may trigger a depression whose cause may be challenging to identify. By removing items previously believed to be necessary, we may disclose extra space (as big as a room or small as a corner) to fashion as our own. Upon transferring only a few treasured objects into our newly adapted area, we welcome newfound simplicity.

Simplicity facilitates an improved environment
where my health will flourish.

June 19

I never promised you a rose garden.

—Hannah Green

Being discontented with relationships increases stress levels and can lead to emotional and physical complications. Any dissatisfaction can result in perhaps seeing only the thorns amidst the roses in our lives. Just as chronic illness has its ups and downs, we can acknowledge that our friends and family have their own challenges.

Most relationships concerning the medically challenged will bloom at their best when we acknowledge our condition without lingering there. We can shift the emphasis from the negative to the positive, helping us view our "garden" in a new light.

Taking a break when we are maxed out is a beneficial way to calm down and regenerate. Gazing beyond our troubles and focusing on the positive allows us to grow abundantly with hope.

Today my focus will be on the blossoms,
not the thorns.

June 20

Every morning is a fresh beginning. Every day is the world made new.

—Dan Custer

We often desire a do-over as chronic health issues apply pressure and daily maintenance develops into a steep mountain we struggle to scale. When fatigue is pronounced, the simple feat of lifting our arm to comb our hair can feel like lifting a hundred-pound weight. Daily chores such as showering can periodically leave us exhausted.

We may begin to realize a different approach is necessary to propel us through our days, and by applying alterations in our schedules and tasks, we actively seize control of the situation. One beneficial change could be introducing moments of relaxation into our day.

If we are experiencing a day of fatigue, let's find a location to sit in the open air and benefit from our expanded vista, delaying more challenging activities to wrestle with at another interval. By accepting each moment for what it is—simply a moment that will soon pass—we free ourselves from undue pressure.

I will realize this day of fresh opportunities.

June 21

In June as many as a dozen species may burst their buds on a single day. No man can heed all of these anniversaries; no man can ignore all of them.

—Aldo Leopold

Summer is that time in my neighborhood when I can enjoy the prolific colorful flowers in addition to a mulberry tree hanging heavy with fruit. I can walk in the dappled light in awe under a grove of southern magnolias, enveloped in their intoxicating beauty. Later I can catch the pungent scent of an oakleaf hydrangea or the sweet fragrance of black locust racemes seemingly dripping from the trees, and all the while my many feathered friends are busy with their serenades.

Even in inclement weather, we can venture outdoors for perhaps a moment, breathing freely, absorbing the sights and sounds of the season. God gave us the diversity of terrain so we would have an enormous, exciting playground. He gave us four seasons so we could admire the flora and fauna that each sustains. Are we grateful for his gifts?

For those of us with health issues, the clarity of our natural world can often take on more significant meaning, as well as healing properties. As we journey outdoors today, let's pause and stop, look, and listen—stopping to be able to enjoy more thoroughly, looking at our surroundings (as one who is new to the area), and listening to any pleasurable sounds our ears may perceive.

Nature's beauty will enhance my life.

June 22

If you don't like something change it; if you can't change
it, change the way you think about it.

—Mary Engelbreit

We may be aware of a myriad of actions or remedies essential for pain relief,
although we may resist change when in the throes of severe pain. If we
focus on soreness and other symptoms, anxiety is the result, which in turn
leads to amplified aching. Believing that a decrease in our pain is possible
can often break the pain cycle and inspire beneficial healing.

To soften its impact, we can try keeping the emphasis away from
the unpleasant symptoms and putting more importance on the positive
aspects of our lives. If perchance pain ramps back up, we can implement
steady breathing, prayer, biofeedback, meditation, or another alternative
relaxation technique. Before you know it, we may note a permanent
decrease in tension-related soreness.

Receiving therapeutic massage has continually been cited as helpful
for chronic pain. The treatment pressure should be matched to our level
of sensitivity at that moment, rendering therapeutic touch healing and
comfortable. Any supportive action we initiate can promote our well-
being, which can be a foundation for self-healing.

I am responsible for my healing.

June 23

It doesn't matter what you write in a journal. It matters that it is yours.

—Sark

Keeping a journal is a suggested tool for chronic illness/pain patients. Jotting down our daily thoughts and concerns provides a means of tracking moods, progress, and the numerous hurdles we encounter. Noting our ideas can be a great release of emotions, and we may see patterns emerge. Our handwriting could differ slightly from page to page, depending on what views we are conveying at the moment. There conceivably might be days of fatigue where we manage merely to note only a sentence or two.

When writing about troubling events, our penmanship may become slightly illegible and possibly include more misspelled words. If anger surfaces, we might notice our strokes growing larger and bolder, perhaps even indenting the paper. Our thoughts of gratitude may bring about a flowing script.

No plan is necessary. Merely putting pen to paper can be a coping mechanism that induces healing. When looking back on these past feelings, we may be surprised by our growth and begin to anticipate further revelations.

I will begin a journal with honesty,
remembering that it is for my eyes only.

June 24

The true object of all human life is play.
—Gilbert. K. Chesterton

It was summer and steamy. I intended to walk (for exercise) in a large, climate-controlled store nearby. After stopping to admire a display of miniature music boxes, I turned the crank on one. Listening to the sweet music rising from the tiny music box left me mesmerized. Continuing to turn the handle, oh, yes, "Gently down the stream" was playing out in my head. It was the "Row, Row, Row Your Boat" melody. *How appropriate,* I thought. This tune was a gentle reminder to keep a lighthearted approach to my life.

There are stints when God leads us to lay aside pain and troubles, freeing ourselves to merely enjoy. Why do some adults stop playing? Having fun can bring on smiles and laughter, producing pain-diminishing endorphins that cause aching to subside.

Play involves an element of fun—the sillier, the better. Uncomplicated card games are terrific, where the focus is on fun, not competition. Encouraging ourselves to concentrate on the enjoyable can make recreation a part of who we are and is healthy and healing. We are all God's children; when life gets difficult, we may need his gentle nudge to replace our struggles with enjoyment.

I will delight in a fun type of play today.

June 25

Weather is uncontrollable. Only the Lord above can control the weather. Whatever we get, we have to work with.

—Maurice Greene

Most of us have probably experienced the unpleasantness of a mosquito bite. Mosquitoes are one of the few bugs that warn us they are coming by buzzing, and in some people, they leave behind an itchy lump. Their buzz is reminiscent of a warning some of us receive when changes in weather or barometric pressure emerge. We may suddenly experience confusion due to fibro fog before precipitation arrives and may feel pain at some point.

When atmospheric pressure drops, minor aches can rapidly turn debilitating. We often tense with the sensations of approaching weather. Our warning or "buzzing" can be the confusion of fibro fog, and this tightening of muscles only increases our level of discomfort. Acknowledging changes in pressure due to weather without giving them the power to dominate our thoughts provides healthier management of our symptoms and, frequently, a decrease in pain levels.

As I understand my symptoms and their effects on me,
I am better able to cope.

June 26

Not everything that is faced can be changed. But nothing can be changed until it is faced.

—James Baldwin

We may encounter people struggling with chronic illness who lament, "Why me?" Some might even be angry with God for their condition. Frustration and anger may be justified, but to blame our physical maladies on anyone (even ourselves) is not. How many of us have blamed ourselves, buying into something we may have heard?

It's not our fault!

Let's ask ourselves what we can do to improve the quality of the present situation. A few possibilities are locating a support group, starting a group ourselves, or looking into counseling, preferably with someone who has experience helping those with chronic pain and illness.

If we desire change in our situation after tiring of the endless days of frustration, anger, and other negative feelings, we first must recognize we may need guidance and support to help get on a more positive wavelength. As we become proactive in our care, we begin steering our thinking away from blame to acceptance, possibilities, and the beginning of our wellness track.

I will evoke positive influences to make way for healthy acceptance.

June 27

Do I contradict myself?
Very well, then I contradict myself.
I am large; I contain multitudes.

—Walt Whitman

From time to time, everyone has confusion. By approaching life with a tolerance of our snafus, we remain more accepting of our many layers. There will be occasions when retreating from a conversation may be wisest because of our confusion. Without being harsh with ourselves, we recognize we are doing our best. It's valuable if we are to be comfortable when communicating with others, having the freedom to be ourselves, including our moments of mistakes and of clarity.

It can be challenging to engage in stimulating conversations and persist in learning and reading thought-provoking material. By striving for a balance of work and recreation, we prompt our brains to continue processing new information. Rather than retreating from the world, we can adapt by facing our fibro fog hurdles.

I will greet the world, accepting my confusion
and welcoming my many lucid moments.

June 28

Wherever you go, no matter what the weather, always bring your own sunshine.

—Anthony J. D'Angelo

The day we discover our responsibility for ourselves—including our reactions to situations—we begin to feel a sense of empowerment. The day we begin practicing this technique, we can realize growth in grace and spirit. No one can rain on our parade unless we permit it.

When arduous individuals adversely affect our lives, try following the saying, "shake it off." If you were to attend a little league game, it's common to hear the coach telling team members when they strike out or miss a catch to "Shake it off." This attitude seems to work well for them, and it can work for us in kind.

One of the best sources of personal sunlight is our smiles. Sure, there are uncertain stretches and days when we don't feel well and smiling seems strained. However, times like these are when smiling is most useful—when we are in our lowest moods. We have a superior self-help coping tool available. It is delightful the way merely smiling can elevate our dispositions, lower pain, and generally make the disagreeable agreeable.

I will carry my own sunshine—in the form of a smile.

June 29

You know, a dog can snap you out of any kind of bad
mood that you're in
faster than you can think of.

—Jill Abramson

As I paused during my park stroll to sit on a welcoming bench, my thoughts swiftly turned gloomy. Then, up bounded a puppy, joyfully tugging his laughing owners with his leash. They asked if I would like to greet their pup. I jumped at the opportunity to engage in all that positivity. Shortly I continued my walk and noted a much-needed lift in my spirits.

When we catch ourselves stumbling toward irritability or stuck in its mire, we have choices. Yes, it is common for people with health challenges to be moody and downright challenging now and again. But this does not make it healthy to remain that way. Just being in proximity to a pet is an easy self-help strategy for improving attitudes. It is hard to be in anything other than pleasant spirits after hugging or interacting with a dog or cat.

No pet? We can purchase a large stuffed animal (no care required) big enough to get our arms around and hug the comforting softness. Keep it somewhere easy to pick up and cuddle often. An uplifted mood can take the bite out of our many impediments while encouraging a healthier lifestyle and the mellowing of our dispositions.

I will seek companionship with a fur baby
to boost my flagging spirits.

June 30

If you're going through hell, keep going.
—Winston Churchill

The knowledge that we have fibromyalgia, an illness with a chronic prognosis, tends to reflect in our attitudes toward any project or relationship we endeavor. By moving ahead in activities despite pain, confusion, and other symptoms, we open the door to progress.

Being overwhelmed with daily activities is a common symptom of our syndrome. Knowing when to rest and when to carry on is a skill gained over time. By setting realistic, obtainable goals, we assist in gleaning hopeful attitudes while pushing past hurdles of often debilitating symptoms. Our lives are overflowing with struggles of various degrees. How we approach them determines whether we overdo it physically and mentally.

When we maintain a positive outlook when facing struggles, whether with illness or in other aspects of our lives, this takes the bite out of some of the most challenging situations, boosting us toward accomplishments.

I will have the courage to handle overwhelming situations
and seek my own successes daily.

July 1

Still round the corner there may wait, a new road or a
secret gate.

—J. R. R. Tolkien

Not giving up the pursuit for optimal health in the face of controversy over
fibromyalgia can be testing if we extract only the negatives concerning our
chronic medical condition. Some physicians fail to recognize it as a valid
condition, and even though fibromyalgia has had a diagnostic billable
code since 2015, it continually is disregarded or considered a "wastebasket
diagnosis" by many healtcare professionals.

As we pursue a means to ease ourselves through this pain and fog that
presses on our lives daily, keeping upbeat whenever possible is essential.
By remaining receptive to advancements in medication and therapies,
whether conventional or alternative, we may feel an unburdening in some
fashion. Our proposed aim can lead to new optimistic roads that branch
off toward wellness, paths that generate hope in lives permanently altered
by diagnosis. We can attempt an altered favorable direction, which can
be productive and encouraging. Through the exploration of any recent
medical findings concerning our illness, we can frequently bring to light
helpful techniques that could soften the damaging effects of chronic
pain—so essential to keeping hope flourishing.

I will try a new, active road toward wellness.

July 2

Never work before breakfast; if you have to work before
breakfast, eat your breakfast first.
> —Josh Billings

It is morning again, that often-dreaded period. And I am frustrated by
waking once more in a state of pain and fatigue. As I crawl out of bed, my
body needs to adjust to simple things, like moving my limbs! I save bathing
until I am more awake. Choosing a no-fuss breakfast helps me to slip into
my day. Beginning the day is frequently my biggest hurdle.

Morning is often a harsh occasion. We may be stiff, sore, and often
worn out from a restless night. Once we accomplish the out-of-bed routine,
we can pat ourselves on the back. It can be a struggle to achieve restorative
sleep. It's always seemingly just beyond our reach. There may be additional
complications, such as obstructive sleep apnea or restless leg syndrome.
Obtaining a diagnosis for these conditions is recommended. Physicians
can then prescribe CPAP therapy, medication, or recommend nutritional
supplements to increase sleep quality.

Our symptoms of irritable bowel syndrome might turn meals in general
into a challenge. Let's consider having a protein fruit smoothie (adhering
to any food sensitivities), one of many hassle-free nutritious choices to
launch our day. Removing the complexity from morning routines through
eating before attempting other tasks can boost our energy before we begin
our day.

I will tweak my schedule, creating stress-free mornings.

July 3

Those who dream by day are cognizant of many things
which escape those who dream only by night.
                                        —Edgar Allen Poe

Let's try an awareness technique to aid in relaxation: sit comfortably
somewhere and do nothing. Just sit there. After a minute or two, we will
probably notice that our minds are roaming. We can relax and flow with
our thoughts; they may settle soon. If we are anxious and do not acquire
the desired result with ease, let's not give up. We can shake out our arms,
rotate our necks, take a few measured breaths, and attempt it once more.
Often simply dreaming by day can reward us with relaxation, creativity,
and renewed energy.

   If we are practicing this exercise daily at approximately the same time,
it can become a coping tool. Unlike meditation, daydreaming can be
carried out anywhere and briefly with our eyes open. Noting our thoughts
gives us information about ourselves. As we resume our activities, we can
perceive any changes in how we feel and acknowledge increases in our
awareness.

While allowing my creative thoughts to ramble,
I will relax for a minimum of fifteen minutes today.

July 4

Use what talents you possess; the woods would be very
silent if no birds sang there except those who sang best.
—Henry Van Dyke

Whatever our talents prediagnosis, we can continue to pursue them
(adjusting our abilities as necessary) while letting go of expectations and
comparisons to prior good health. Continuing to enjoy our skills can
lend us pleasure if we cease judging or equating our results with those of
anyone—even ourselves.

We can go outdoors and listen to birdcalls. It might require us to
travel to an area such as a park to hear our feathered friends. When we are
listening, we may pick up the melodies of many different bird songs, all
beautiful in their own right. Even a crow's call lends balance to the trill of
smaller songbirds, such as the yellow finch. Notice how each bird makes its
specific music and does not copy another species (mockingbirds being the
exception). The various warbles of different avian species are our reminder
that everyone has talents and to utilize what gifts we possess is a move in
a positive direction.

I will spread my wings, singing my own song.

July 5

We attract what we habitually expect; we become what
we deeply believe.

—William Arthur Ward

We reveal the power of the human mind to shape our reality if we
continually expect the worst and then complain when we get precisely
that. This can result in unhelpful beliefs that could etch into our psyches.
It may take a strong sense of self to dispel an image that we are undeserving
of better things, such as improved health and greater happiness.

Knowing control over our actions and reactions is favorable, we
can strive for an encouraging approach to chronic medical problems. If
possible, let's limit the emphasis on the drawbacks of any health diagnosis.

By taking stock of what we are inviting into our lives, our question may
be, "What do I desire for my life presently?" Then, while trusting ourselves
to expect improvements in well-being, we may be led to wiser impending
choices, such as a calm environment in which to heal and the gift of a few
good friends along the way.

Today I will have a good day.

July 6

We all want to help one another. Human beings are like that. We want to live by each other's happiness, not by each other's misery.

—Charlie Chaplin

But what about our misery? Life isn't all rosebuds and rainbows, although it is unnecessary to divulge our gloomy details to others. Asking for help can become problematic, and we may feel that depending on others will weaken our sense of self-reliance. There is a delicate balance to acknowledge when we need assistance and recognizing when to go it alone. Yearning to maintain a modicum of independence can produce a hesitancy to call upon another. But as we attempt to help others whenever possible, it becomes more tolerable to lean on them occasionally.

The giving and receiving of support is a common occurrence, especially among those with health challenges. Having someone to telephone to share good news or meet for a relaxing get-together can assist us in communication and connection.

When happiness is abundant, we can share it with others, paying it forward. Learning to plot a course through life's ups and downs takes practice, and occasionally help is necessary. Finding a balance between healthy independence and sporadic assistance (while sharing the pleasant whenever possible) is something to aspire to.

I will reach out and connect with someone today.

July 7

The key is not to prioritize what's on your schedule, but to schedule your priorities.

—Stephen R. Covey

Presently, we may have countless days with a conceived plan that goes nowhere, and we might have a yearning to relinquish scheduling, for our bodies and symptoms periodically make their own agendas. By establishing some breathing room in our daily calendars, we create the variance between a great day and a grueling one, lessening any pressure on ourselves. When we are checking on any arrangements we made with others, it is worthwhile to take our abilities into account and schedule moment to moment.

By carving out periods to relax and play—positioning these as a top priority—we hold stress to a minimum. If our plans include others, informing them of any limitations in advance eliminates the chance of disappointments (should the agenda change unexpectedly because of our symptoms). When we are journeying out, it is valuable to remember our energy requirements for the trip back. Prearranging return transportation if necessary can be a wise choice. By maintaining a flexible routine, we remain in control of our syndrome instead of it controlling us.

I will set aside some breathing room in my schedule today.
The result is flexibility.

July 8

Adventure is worthwhile in itself.

—Amelia Earhart

I was flying high among the seagulls! Relishing the feeling of a few raindrops colliding with me before cascading toward their destination—the sparkling blue sea below—I laughed once again. From the moment the parasail caught the wind and lifted me in a sling-type apparatus from the speedboat, I was hooting and whooping it up in sheer delight! Yes, my hip tender points were in a painful squeeze, but I was awash with exhilaration from dipping and swaying in the breeze while drinking in the spectacular view of my incredible adventure.

Have we assembled a want-to-do-someday list? Some may refer to it as a bucket list. A principal reason to list some of the more outlandish desires is that they may be possible. Sure, it's difficult merely walking on certain days. But that does not mean we should stop dreaming of beckoning adventures. A majority of theme parks have rides for physically challenged people if assistance is required. Anything that lets us set our symptoms aside and experience elation for a few minutes is worth effort and exploration.

I will answer the call of adventure
with enthusiasm and delight.

July 9

Anger is not an independent emotion,
behind it stands either frustration, worry, or hurt.
                                        —Tanna Horton

Those who are chronically ill may feel more frustration and anger than other people. Displaying our anger can conceivably cause lapses in communication, and we can create additional health problems for ourselves, such as a risk of hypertension.

We can try these healthy coping methods when we are experiencing anger: listing everything that infuriates us and then tearing up the list; going out in nature for a walk, giving us a new perspective; doing something physical, like sweeping floors, folding clothes, or picking flowers; or calling a friend and talking about pleasantries.

Somewhere in between an excessive display of emotional anger and stuffing our anger down is a good place to land. Being aware and in control of our emotions can be a challenging, though worthwhile, endeavor.

Anger does not empower me;
however, control over my emotions does.

July 10

To possess ideas is to gather flowers; to think is to weave
them into garlands.
—Anne-Sophie Swetchine

There may be occasions when our thinking—threaded with fibro fog—
causes our weaving of thoughts to take on the look of an ill-matched
patchwork quilt. We can give our brains a nudge by compiling a list
consisting of names of our closest neighbors, their children, and their
pets with a brief description. Consider making a notation of personal
and business contacts, along with the names and telephone numbers
of physicians, including medical assistants, nurse practitioners, and
receptionists, because although today we may remember their monikers,
tomorrow we may not.

Before leaving for an appointment, we can refresh our memories
with the correct names, including directions. For those daily errands
and appointments, it can be helpful to use different-colored sticky notes
outlining the chores or errands we need to do. Any action that enables our
thinking process can be an asset in preventing fibro fog from dominating,
creating a favorable place for thoughts to bloom.

I will gather ideas as they blossom,
assisting my fibro fog moments.

July 11

Let us be grateful to people who make us happy; they are
the charming gardeners who make our souls blossom.
—Jacques Prevert

We are fortunate if we are acquainted with people who inspire us to be
upbeat and cheerful regardless of the sort of day we are having. It could be
a family member or a special friend who sees a flower in us, where another
may perceive only a weed. Those who provoke a smile or laugh are a gift
to our souls, aiding us through the taxing intervals and those in-between
periods.

Let's cherish those extraordinary individuals whose belief in us is
constant and unwavering. A telephone call or a note thanking them for
boosting our spirits with their encouraging attitudes may be overdue.
By resisting depending solely on others for our happiness and relishing
any pleasantness when we bump into it, we encourage active wellness
development. Similarly, seizing an opportunity to give back any cheerfulness
shown to us continues spreading seeds of delight.

I will bloom gratefully in the happiness I am gifted.

July 12

All our progress is an unfolding, like the vegetable bud, you
have first an instinct, then an opinion, then a knowledge,
as the plant has root, bud and fruit. Trust the instinct to
the end, though you can render no reason.

—Ralph Waldo Emerson

Of course, we desire to progress in all aspects of our lives. However, the
method we choose when formulating improvements can alter depending
on the circumstances. Accordingly, there may be no rhyme or reason
to what we feel is a superior way, merely a gut feeling—something that
just feels right. By trusting our instincts, we can become empowered
and replace despondency with confidence while arming ourselves with
knowledge.

Having the self-assurance to follow through with individual judgments
can be risky (if we are only going on instinct). But we have opinions and
awareness to support our decisions, leading to another step in unfolding
toward progress and a sense of well-being. Through being cognizant of our
options and standing firm in our choices, any progress we acquire can be
considered a success.

I will trust my instincts.

July 13

True hope dwells on the possible, even when life seems to be a plot written by someone who wants to see how much adversity we can overcome.

—Walter Anderson

There can be moments when we may think that our health or symptoms could not get any worse. Let's view our possibilities for a moment, turning our attention to what we have achieved. Are we able to walk outdoors, if only for a few minutes? Perhaps we have joined water aerobics or a gentle exercise class (stretching and strengthening muscles can minimize pain). How about moods? Have we gained some control over them? By being conscious of our flare up triggers and acquiring an attitude of hope as a buffer toward the taxing aspects of each day, our symptoms and outlooks can improve.

As we overcome our physical adversities (no matter how small or insignificant), our reward is freedom of movement, opening us to a more extensive range of activities. We begin to realize a possibility and then another possibility. Subsequently, we do not judge ourselves by our misfortunes so much as by our accomplishments. By exiting the realm of self-imposed exile that can arrive with chronic illness, we attain new beginnings and new hope.

I will embrace life with hope today.

July 14

I've always enjoyed things going at a nice pace, nothing too fast, nothing too crazy.

—Thomas Luther Bryan

On one of my journeys, I was experiencing a flare up due to severe fatigue resulting from a lack of sleep the first night and subsequent nights. On the return flight, it quickly became, "hurry, hurry, rush, rush," requiring me to use an assistive device because I was incapable of navigating the sea of people in the bustling airport. I realized I had allowed myself to be sleep deprived, and my fatigue was not lifting. Collapsing in a wheelchair and resigning to being propelled through the crowded terminal, I resolved to approach my life with more care, guaranteeing the expansion of healthier living.

On occasion, we might have a "whatever it takes" approach to our chronic medical condition. We may find if we overdo it (or allow others to push us) and spiral into a hectic pace, we become overwhelmed, which could result in a flare up. Rest then becomes essential to get us back on track. An advantageous strategy to embrace involves us maintaining an eye on wellness and resolve in pacing. Consider scheduled and impromptu breathers throughout the day (depending on our level of pain and fatigue), not allowing anyone to push us past our physical limits. With a balance of work, entertainment, and rest, we can be rewarded with optimum wellness. Regardless of our daily hurdles, a renewed balance in pacing can restore a sense of ease.

I will benefit from a comfortable pace today.

July 15

Earth and sky, woods and fields, lakes and rivers, the
mountain and the sea, are excellent schoolmasters, and
teach some of us more than we can learn from books.
—Sir John Lubbock

Ever go fishing from a bank or a small boat with just a simple pole? It isn't
the catch that is goal (many follow the catch-and-release method) but the
meditative energy of fishing, daydreaming, and feasibly almost napping
from a combination of fresh air and warm sun flickering off the water.

As thoughts cease to churn and the favorable aspects of outdoors take
hold where anxiety used to dwell, we may notice our breathing leveling
and our muscles becoming relaxed. Let's try venturing into nature and
sitting directly on the ground or upon a fallen log, serenely, with the sole
intent of observation. Perhaps we can attempt a walking meditation, where
our thoughts are only of our surroundings, and we expel any worry or
discontent.

Time appears to halt as we are unencumbered from our cares, relishing
rejuvenation from a possible sinking spirit. Later when we depart, we
restore the area to its former state, preserving the wild beauty therein with
a fresh appreciation of God's gifts and a plan to return once again.

I will go to nature and learn today.

July 16

Nobody sees a flower—really—it is so small it takes time
—we haven't time—and to see takes time, like to have a
friend takes time.

—Georgia O'Keeffe

We can keep our friendships intact while contending with fibromyalgia, but it can be challenging. There is no question that the onslaught of our many symptoms alters us, and learning to carry on while caught up in medical turmoil can take its toll on those who are nearest and dearest.

Those friendships that manage to endure may become fine-tuned by patience, which is obligatory in the face of this baffling condition. We so often must put our needs first. Not everyone may be able to make this arduous journey with us, and this can be a deal-breaker for some. Our agendas could be maxed out, or we may lack the energy to nurture every friendship like we would wish.

We might encounter a mutually supportive and understanding relationship with those also surviving the trials of a chronic health condition. Occasionally someone who shares a similar diagnosis may cross our path, and we can cherish this kindred spirit.

I am grateful for the acquaintance of a friend with a chronic illness.
I call this friendship a special friendship.

July 17

Life isn't about finding yourself. Life is about creating yourself.

—George Bernard Shaw

The phrase "they broke the mold when they made her" usually refers to an individual with truly unique qualities. Our Creator formed each person to be unique and one of a kind. We need only to recognize *who we are.* However, tweaking things a bit and applying some creative improvements to help smooth over any rough edges may be in order.

By what methods are we restored to our best? Some suggestions are to attend a spiritual gathering and dust off our prayer skills, visit a museum exhibit, or watch a sporting event (the one we always dreamed of participating in but cannot). To expand our thinking capabilities, try reading a challenging book or learning new skills. Knowing that what we view or read shapes our thoughts, we may invite some humor or uplifting stories into our existence as well.

I shape my life and paint my future.

July 18

If wrinkles must be written upon our brows, let them not be written upon the heart. The spirit should never grow old.

—John Kenneth Galbraith

Many of the challenging circumstances we encounter during our lives can include undesirable lingering consequences. Sometimes we may feel we are sure to get premature gray hair from all the trials, or with each worrying snag, we find ourselves hunting for a wrinkle on our brow. Struggling with chronic medical problems ought not to develop into worry and stress, although it often does.

Haven't we met individuals whose faces are etched with wisdom, yet whose hearts are carefree and loving? And if so, doesn't it seem like they are capable of smiling and laughing with abandon? These encouraging attitudes could be the hope for our future.

Dwelling on our own or another's dilemmas may leave us at the peril of sinking spirits. We can choose to dismiss pressure that belongs to others, thereby freeing ourselves from unnecessary worry. Accepting current health situations and moving on with our agendas makes for a more relaxed disposition inside and out, preventing life's wrinkles from forming prematurely upon our faces and hearts.

Smiling often during my day prevents tribulations
from sinking my spirits.

July 19

I have sometimes been wildly, despairingly, acutely miserable, but through it all I still know quite certainly that just to be alive is a grand thing.

—Agatha Christie

In adjusting to any chronic illness, accepting the flux and the uncertainty is crucial. In our inner core, we may every so often feel like wailing when facing some of the aspects of our diagnosis. However, positioning our energy to work in productive areas may be more useful. Fibromyalgia with its many symptoms will always be throwing us curves, keeping us on our toes, testing our reserves. Not letting the illness win and realizing tactics to manage symptoms becomes vital for an enriched existence.

We know that we will always have adjustments to make as different symptoms present themselves; this is a form of coping in itself. Flexibility is a great asset when we are learning to adjust to living with a chronic condition. When it comes to fibromyalgia, the ability to accept whatever the day may bring may be a struggle, but it is a prime method of coping.

I will learn a coping skill
to help aid my fibromyalgia wellness plan.

July 20

Peace is not the absence of conflict. It is the ability to handle conflict by peaceful means.

—Ronald Reagan

Conflict happens. Generally, it is the way we manage disagreements that arise now and again that averts eruption into full-fledged anxiety. We can explore some helpful techniques to settle our differences with others.

Often the best approach is a thoughtful timeout from a tense situation. Extracting ourselves, even for a short period, allows space for cool-headed reassessment. Journaling specifics of any difficulty or perceived tension and allowing a day to lapse before we tackle the problem can also be a useful tool. If additional assistance is required, we may seek a third party's perspective or look to a mediator, counselor, or support group. By coping with conflict peacefully, we prevent its negative influence from gaining too much weight in our lives.

I will cope with conflict with a healthy approach
leading to an amplification of peace.

July 21

And the days went by like wind; Everything changed,
then changed again.

—Tom Petty

During my healthier days, before I became personally acquainted with
fibromyalgia, I dreamt of growing my own food—an organic bounty. My
dream became a reality as a small patch of ground designated for my garden
was tilled—only to expose crabgrass roots. The crabgrass stalled my plan
as I applied the painstaking labor of hand sifting the unmanageable roots
from the soil. The planting stage came next. I had such fun choosing fruits
and vegetables to grow. Soon the tiny seedlings changed into blooming
masses. My son Robbie's kindergarten class visited as a field trip where they
roamed the bounty and handpicked and tasted fresh strawberries ripe and
delicious straight from the garden.

What has changed since our diagnosis? How many of our dreams
have we actualized? It is beneficial for us to continue with our hopes and
dreams in the circle of life, even when we are facing the many changes
that a fibromyalgia diagnosis carries. We can grow that garden, paint
that picture, and take that course of our dreams. Create a list of goals to
accomplish, a doable list that allows for our challenges. Life goes on, with
many changes, and we can continually find new ways to achieve success.

I will accept change and flow with it—nature's design.

July 22

Trust that still, small voice that says, "This might work and I'll try it."

—Diane Mariechild

We may speculate, "Will my pain ever end?" The realization that focusing on the unpleasant symptoms of fibromyalgia increases their undesirable hold on us arrives quickly. With the multitude of symptoms facing us every day, we may go about madly searching for relief. Here are some dos and do nots that can be of assistance for ease of everyday living:

- Do not stay in bed.
- Do not over-exercise.
- Do not plan too much in a day.
- Do get enough rest.
- Do stretch and take leisurely walks.
- Do take some periods off to do nothing.
- Do take warm water soaks or showers.

I will formulate a plan for coping with my symptoms.

July 23

Patience with others is Love. Patience with self is Hope.
Patience with God is Faith.

—Adel Bestavros

Everything we understand about having patience we can practice daily.
Perhaps we must wait for our children who are attending after-school
programs or experience long delays to see physicians or lining up for public
transit. Taking along a book and earplugs can ease nerves, and our serenity
becomes more attainable when we block excess noise generated by people,
media, or traffic. Exhibiting tolerance within our family when they do not
always get what is going on with us demonstrates the love we feel for them.

Occasionally we may become frustrated when our comprehension
becomes muddled because of the frequently annoying symptom of fibro
fog. Our confusion reminds us once again to be tolerant with ourselves, for
we desire the same consideration and love that we extend to others. With
the knowledge that God has his own timetable, we can apply patience
when we pray, confident of thriving in an atmosphere of hope, love, and
faith.

Patience is an art to practice.

July 24

Live and work but do not forget to play
to have fun in life and really enjoy it.

—Eileen Caddy

"Put on your play clothes!" I remember this cheerful chant from my mother when as youngsters we would return from church or school and be reminded that now we were free to play.

Who permits us to play as adults? We may feel a burden of typical adult responsibilities: perhaps making chores a priority by working into the night, forgetting how to enjoy a weekend, or managing a vacation. Currently, work can follow us wherever we go (if we allow it); it is up to us to say "when."

Grab a friend, family member, or pet and just play, whether inside or outdoors. There's nothing to it but a plethora of laughs and smiles. Keep it light, not competitive. Giving ourselves permission to hang up our work clothes and slip into our play clothes can flip the switch to enjoyment. We no longer are that accountant, mother, teacher, wife—just a person having fun. Years seem to melt away when we regularly engage in playfulness.

I will throw on my "play clothes" and have some fun.

July 25

There is always music amongst the trees in the garden but
our hearts must be very quiet to hear it.

—Minnie Aumonier

When illness seems to pile on tension with pressures mounting daily, we
may seek the best environment to lighten our pain-laden hearts, minds,
and bodies. Allowing for a contented silence in our daily routine can
disclose many a blessing. After much effort in attempting to understand
our diagnosis and fathom our condition, we may discover that the stillness
of nature ushers in the gift of serenity. Even Mother Nature's birds and
trees enjoy an individual visiting them who respects their need for calm.

One of the most beneficial occasions to be in natural surroundings is
when we are experiencing pain. We may be awed by the cadence of crickets
or the whoosh of wind caressing the trees. Although it may be difficult to
dislodge ourselves from a comfortable chair, the health-giving attributes
of walking in the great outdoors are remarkable. When we connect with
the natural treasures found in green spaces, there may be a perception of
a gentle release of pain. This potent ingredient of our healing can be very
gratifying, bearing the power to shift our setbacks into soul-flooding joy.

I will obtain comfort in listening to nature's
magnificent daytime symphonies
or its soothing nighttime melodies.

July 26

Argue for your limitations and sure enough they're yours.
—Richard Bach

Chronic illness can move in and take over the spare room like an uninvited guest. On occasion, we may fall into the habit of focusing on our disabilities rather than our capabilities, although maintaining a positive attitude can be challenging when we are in the middle of a flare up of symptoms.

As an alternative, we could invest our energy in reflecting on our strengths. Those pleasantries in our lives like having a good relationship with friends and family or enjoying a craft or hobby enable the elevation of our moods. By keeping our lives centered on more than our faltering health, we foster growth as an individual. Taking a respite from referring to our aches and pains and observing when the spotlight is off our problems encourages us to highlight the positive aspects of who we are. Smiling becomes effortless, and tension can abate when we shift our emphasis to a constructive subject.

I will reflect on my strengths today.

July 27

The great artist and thinker are the simplifiers.
—Henri Frederic Amiel

During my childhood, meal preparation for my large family was usually a time-consuming project. To simplify matters, my parents served banana splits now and then for Sunday evening meals. This simple change in routines brought an element of fun to dinner. We would each prepare our sugar-laden concoction to our liking using a few essential ingredients. This was probably the only meal when all seven of us agreed on the menu. Years later, on rare occasions, I passed down this simple, pleasurable dinner to my two children, who were also very keen on this fun meal.

Our lives can often get too complicated. And there are days when we can't seem to catch up. Cutting ourselves some slack can be a cushion against being overwhelmed and continually expecting everything to be going splendidly. The desire to have increased ease in some aspects of living is within our control, so let's break a few of our rules on occasion, breathing fresh air into our challenging lives. By embracing our creative aspects, we can introduce a little pleasure and enjoyment into our often humdrum existence. If we lack ideas for simplifying, we could ask our families, and who knows what lightness and fun we can factor into our day!

Out of simplicity, I acquire desirable cheerfulness.

July 28

Tears of joy are like the summer rain drops pierced by sunbeams.

—Hosea Ballou

Have we caught ourselves holding back tears of happiness once again? Perhaps we are feeling the embarrassment of thinking we are overly emotional or conceivably losing control. A sentimental commercial on television, a heartfelt greeting card, attending a wedding, or just looking at two people in love may all inspire tears.

Allowing ourselves to vent our feelings in a healthy way through the sincere expression of joyful tears can be beneficial to our health and well-being. If we shut down our emotions, they could build internally, often escaping in the form of uncontrollable sobs or anger, for seemingly no reason.

Emotional tears (happy or sad) release a protein-based hormone that is a *natural painkiller*. We can regard subsequent feelings that tug at our heartstrings producing tears as beneficial. It is easier to welcome emotive tears of any variety when we bring to mind their healing properties.

I will maintain a healthy outlook toward tears.

July 29

Remember that stress doesn't come from what's going on in your life. It comes from your thoughts about what's going on in your life.

—Andrew Bernstein

Taking a closer look at how we manage our stress levels can be enlightening. Stress may be a symptom of medical issues, but how are we coping with the pressure in our lives? If we tend to magnify our problems out of proportion, we might be holding onto stress-provoking patterns, thereby turning them into nonproductive daily habits. On the other hand, if our anxiety comes from an outside source, such as work, specific people, or certain surroundings, we can try backing away. Our well-being stays intact when we don't allow grievances to enter the picture.

Self-created anxiety can produce a taxing atmosphere that could intensify pain, cause flare ups, and wreak havoc on immune systems by creating a chronic inflammatory condition and lowered immunity. Enhanced health is accessible when we release our grip on worry. We can turn instead to the ability to practice tension relievers, such as deep-breathing techniques and a relaxed pursuit of wellness.

I will release my worries and anxieties today,
thereby improving my health.

July 30

Many can brook the weather that love not the wind.
—William Shakespeare

It was puzzling to me how in hot weather a ceiling fan circulating overhead or an energetic wind outdoors could cause my joints to ache, similar to what I contend with in winter. After discovering that a brisk air current of any variety can cause pain in the sensitive areas, I now wear a cover-up when I encounter fans or air conditioning and am better prepared when I go outdoors. Even in summer, I carry a long-sleeved cotton shirt to use as a cover-up in chilly restaurants, physicians' offices, and friend's homes.

Sensitivities on so many levels can affect us daily. Knowing that we may be affected by winds (from any source) and the pain that it can produce, we can choose our wardrobe accordingly. Wearing layers is recommended for any weather as we can add or remove layers as needed. Also, by investing in neck scarves, vests, and outer garments such as fingerless gloves and wrist warmers, we can achieve comfort indoors or out. If we approach dressing in this way, it enables us to face the breeze of any variety and be comfortable.

I will ensure my comfort daily.

July 31

My advice to you is not to inquire why or whither, but just enjoy your ice cream while it is on your plate—that's my philosophy.

—Thornton Niven Wilder

There may be days that sing with contentment and delight—when physical discomfort or other disagreeable symptoms are absent or diminished and not intruding into our schedules. Perhaps we are so familiar with the reverse situation that we do not trust when things are going swimmingly.

We can get in a rut—always assuming the going will be rough. And this type of thinking prepares us for trying intervals but leaves us deficient at recognizing the excellent, even when it is directly before us.

When an excellent day unfolds, let's welcome it with a relaxed approach and a wealth of smiles, not questioning, "How could this be?" but saying instead, "I'll take it!" When we are blessed with such a day, we can approach these gifts by relishing every ounce of pleasure and satisfaction we encounter with beaming attitudes and heaps of gratitude.

I will grab my spoon before my ice cream melts and dig in.

August 1

It is difficult to say what is impossible, for the dream of
yesterday is the hope of today and the reality of tomorrow.
—Robert H. Goddard

For chronic illness patients, hope can be what helps us arise in the morning.
It can be our shield from despair, which can cloud our often-shrouded view
of the world. And what motivates us, for the most part, can also be hope,
for without it many of us would have given up, letting our syndrome cast
an ominous shadow upon our lives—and our dreams.

   A life without hope is a life without a vision or purpose. There will be
days of flare ups and symptoms that seem unrelenting. That's when we can
put one foot in front of the other and hope for a better tomorrow. Who's
to say what is possible. We must allow ourselves permission to feel whole,
to feel there is indeed a glimmer of a chance that we will be able to go on,
making it through one more day, for this is the essence of hope.

I will introduce myself to hope today.

August 2

The only normal people are those you don't know very well.

—Foe Ancis

This striving to be "normal" is often overrated. If we bear in mind that everyone is unique (in their own way), we realize there is no normal. Let's drop our quest for normalcy and welcome fun in our day instead.

We could try some amusing activities where fun becomes our only objective. Who knows—they might become a favorite means of relaxing. Remember those bottles of bubbles with a wand inside to blow or wave that we may rationalize are for children? We can buy a bottle. Now prepare to have some merriment with them in daylight or even night, with only moon or streetlight illuminating their iridescence as they float and collide in the air. This delightful activity can be enjoyed alone as a pick-me-up or as a relaxation tool when we are feeling overwrought. Try grabbing a friend and sharing the happy experience. Caution, giggles are contagious.

We can place the bubble container on a visible counter to prompt us to take a bit of diversion now and again. This fun activity is guaranteed to bring smiles of joy if not laughter, which are so welcome in our often pain-racked bodies. Later we can explore additional activities without concern about whether they are customary purely for the joy they generate.

I will forget "normal" today and aim for fun.

August 3

The simplification of life is one of the steps to inner peace.
A persistent simplification will create an inner and outer
well-being that places harmony in one's life.

—Peace Pilgrim

Living with a chronic medical problem has the potential to undo even the strongest of individuals. It is how we react to our symptoms and present lives in general that prompts our sense of well-being. We may find ourselves either overdoing activities or raising the bar on our hurdles, generating even more obstacles. Or could we be doing the opposite, resting all day and then wondering why we feel so poorly and have difficulty sleeping at night?

Stumbling blocks such as annoying symptoms or anxious circumstances are most easily dealt with one by one. We can ease up on ourselves by discovering how to live an uncomplicated life, reducing those must-do lists and providing a glimpse of the inner peace we may crave. Through not projecting our failures and accepting the way things are, we can create lasting internal and external calm. The most challenging situations can improve along with our emotional well-being.

I will seek harmony in my life by indulging in simplification,
thereby creating inner peace.

August 4

That man is happiest who lives from day to day and asks
no more, garnering the simple goodness of life.

—Euripides

It may not be our usual pattern to live day to day, taking each twenty-four hours as it unfolds—not forcing what occurs, accepting everything as is. If we tend to over-plan and maintain rigid schedules, this can cause increased fatigue and tension. Making decisions on what to let go and what requires our attention can be unfamiliar and confusing. But through this means, we encourage effortlessness in our every day.

There can be occasions when rearranging our plans and flowing with life provide a more natural course. As we begin to encourage flexibility in our schedules and routines, we free up intervals to embrace something enjoyable (not necessarily complicated or elaborate). We can profit significantly from an hour of unplanned, upbeat activity (begin weekly and aim for daily), thereby easing our burdens and obstacles. A reduction of everyday hassles that are present in our lives is attainable when we enjoy the advantages and ease of spirit—through the adoption of an uncomplicated way of living.

Effortlessness in life keeps me truly happy.

August 5

It is the marriage of the soul with Nature that makes the
intellect fruitful, and gives birth to imagination.
                                        —Henry David Thoreau

Come with me on an imaginative walk ...

Let's clear our heads and leave all health issues behind. As we step
outdoors in our imaginations and welcome the pleasing, fresh air with a
lightness of spirit, we follow a sun-dappled, wooded path, stopping to pick
plump, wild blackberries, juices trickling down our chins. Continuing on,
we notice a jeweled butterfly joining us on our trek. A mockingbird trills a
hello as we pass beneath a towering oak. We arrive at a meadow sprinkled
with an abundance of wildflowers, and while pausing to gather a few, we
breathe in, enveloping the smells and sounds of the terrain. All too quickly,
it is time to turn around, taking the memory of our mental picture outing
to call upon at will.

From time to time, let's relish a fictional visit to Mother Nature with
her legendary beauty and superb tranquility. Our visionary stroll can
provide an occasion for exploration and discovery. By using our sense of
innovation, we can expand our lives and comfort ourselves even on our
worst of days. To reach beyond borders of health issues and grasp expansive
images of an inventive trip to nature can be a novel and reassuring
experience. Learning to turn away from tasks and errands and soak up
dreams from the natural world to revisit at our leisure soothes any anxiety
and increases our imaginations.

I will bring forth a golden image from nature
to cope with my symptoms.

August 6

Motivation is what gets you started. Habit is what keeps
you going.
—Jim Ryun

Exercise is beneficial for everyone. Although we may be challenged to adapt
to a regular exercise program or discover moderate physical movements
that most suit our capabilities, it can be a valuable goal.

Getting outdoors is easy for many; for others, it may be hard to pull
ourselves out of that comfortable chair. As we appreciate the advantages of
walking daily and the influence it has on our well-being and stress levels,
this may be ample motivation to initiate a walking routine. Let's begin
leisurely with just a stroll, not forcing anything. If we are unaccustomed
to walking or any exercise, we can keep it to five minutes at the start and
gradually increase the time. With a little determination and motivated by
improvements in mood and pain, walking may become a favored pastime.

If the weather is foul, we could walk indoors. Walking is an activity
where we get to choose our setting. We can walk alone, with another
person, or with a pet. By looking forward to our daily stride, it no longer
feels like exercise, only intervals well spent.

I will carve out minutes in my day for walking
while enjoying my surroundings.

August 7

Comedy is defiance. It's a snort of contempt in the face of fear and anxiety. And it's the laughter that allows hope to creep back on the inhale.

—Will Durst

Here it comes again: that gripping feeling that indicates all is not well. During these times, our breathing may become difficult or shallow. We may even hold our breath unknowingly. Anxiety can be a crippling companion to chronic medical problems.

When never-ending symptoms have stirred up feelings that we can't go on and we seem to have lost hope, this is when we might try lightening up. By distracting ourselves with pleasurable thoughts, our anxiety can diminish. We can observe the ridiculous and silly that is always at hand and laugh aloud.

Life is for living, and we need not be anxious or fearful. Inviting a little laughter into every day can erase those frown lines, appease that apprehension, relax those muscles, and lessen any perceived pain.

I will enjoy a laugh today,
diminishing my unease while breathing hope back into my heart.

August 8

Just don't give up trying to do what you really want to do. Where there is love and inspiration, I don't think you can go wrong.

—Ella Fitzgerald

Whether our interest is in art, singing, science, storytelling, or one of many possible pursuits, the desire to forge ahead is noble. Diminished health may steal numerous capabilities; however, other talents that might have lain dormant may now have an opportunity to shine.

Several of us may be tempted to give up cherished activities after having our world change so dramatically with various encumbering symptoms. Being active, especially in something we enjoy, can distract us from health issues and make the day more tolerable. And our love of a specific pursuit can transcend any accompanying challenges that ensue, leaving bare the essence of inspiration.

Today I will draw a picture,
sew a simple pattern, or do something else I love.

August 9

Fall seven times, stand up eight.

—Japanese proverb

We hope never to experience a fall. But if we have the misfortune of taking a spill, retaining a record of the events that led to the stumble and any injury that transpired can be revealing. By maintaining a log of any falls, we can determine if we are striving to achieve physical endeavors beyond our capabilities. If any bodily injury or pain occurs, a physician may recommend physical therapy to assist with a speedy mending. And following through with a suggestion of PT can hasten our healing, help strengthen any weakened muscles, and relax any taut muscles.

Repeatedly taxing our bodies beyond their limits could cause painful repercussions, such as muscle tension, cramps, or damage to tendons and ligaments. Through the application of brief, gentle stretching before walking or exercising, we can help protect ourselves from harm.

We may have heard the phrase "bounce back from injuries," although for those of us with physical limitations, this is not always readily achievable. Any strain to our bodies can heap further impairment on our already compromised immune systems. It doesn't matter how slow we are moving; it only matters that we are moving!

With gratitude, I will enjoy a walk today.

August 10

When faced with a mountain, I will not quit! I will keep on striving until I climb over, find a pass through, tunnel underneath, or simply stay and turn the mountain into a gold mine—with God's help!

—Robert Schuller

Surely, fibromyalgia is a mountain. It is described as a mysterious syndrome sometimes triggered by an initial trauma, which indicates many patients diagnosed have had accidents and misfortune in our lives. Very often, our first response to diagnosis is *no*. Who would want this? Or we might be relieved that the multitude of symptoms we have been experiencing finally have a name.

After the initial shock or resignation period has worn off, we are left to get on with our changed lives. As we oversee our well-being and daily lifestyles and assume a proactive role in our wellness, enhanced mental, physical, and spiritual health emerges. Transforming chronic illness into anything positive might be unthinkable for some—although when we consider the ways it has opened our minds and hearts, we may reconsider. Let's continue to thank God wherever we are in our goal toward a healthier life and ask his blessings for ourselves and others with chronic illness.

I will not quit.

August 11

Put duties aside at least one hour before bed and perform
soothing quiet activities that will help you relax.
—Dianne Hales

Do we require permission to relax? Possibly. Typically, we might rationalize
the necessity of tackling many late-day tasks instead of easing into relaxation
for the evening. There is an agreement that exercise (while beneficial) is
best when carried out earlier, no closer than two to three hours before
bedtime. Winding down at least an hour before bed can facilitate better
quality sleep. If we retire to a quiet area out of a noisy environment, rest
is encouraged. We can adopt a soothing nocturnal routine and healthy
sleep habits.

A few ideas for relaxing are coloring, needlework, or any activity that
is calming; some may enjoy a warm bath, while others settle down with
soothing music or light reading—all contributing to a restful regimen.
The value of establishing a nightly ritual signals the body that it is time
for sleep. Apart from improved rest, setting aside time for ourselves near
bedtime improves our attitudes and dispositions, in addition to lowering
stress, all necessary to maintaining a health-giving lifestyle.

I will implement a relaxation routine beginning tonight.

August 12

Many waters cannot quench love, neither can the floods drown it …

— Song of Solomon 8:7

Countless sources have attempted to explain the meaning of love, yet it remains a mystery. There are many types of love: romantic, friendship, caring, concern, paternal, and so forth. All love is thoughtful and supportive. The affection we feel for friends is not all-consuming, and it should not be demanding or draining. The love we feel for our children is unconditional. This love can be constant, even when our kids have grown and moved on.

If we are fortunate enough to find real, healthy, lasting romantic love that thrives past the initial attraction and develops into mature love, this is a gift to treasure. This emotion flourishes with nourishment and protection, and it can be fragile and demanding at times.

We can aim to keep a balance between caring for others and caring for ourselves (self-love). An upset in this balance can bring on tension and cause more harm to our already sensitive systems. So, let's love with abandon, garnering the benefits.

I will love myself, creating a firm foundation for loving others.

August 13

Your calm mind is the ultimate weapon against your
challenges. So relax.
                                                    —Bryant McGill

Several years ago I resided alone in a small coastal town. My cottage stood
on a quiet street surrounded by live oaks and other large shade trees. I
have fond recollections of sitting near a rear window and gazing upon my
shaded backyard, neither reading nor talking on the telephone, merely
sitting and enjoying my view. Birds and rabbits loved my serene backyard
and hopped over near the low window where I relaxed. I even had the rare
glimpse of a neighbor's two peacocks out for a stroll.

Sitting by a window and delighting in whatever season can be very
soothing. While engaged in this form of meditation, we hold the symptom
of anxiety at bay. Let's try relaxing in any room with a window, where we
can observe and enjoy the scene. Even resting quietly in a place without
much of a view can be peaceful. It is of note that people recovering from
surgery have fewer complications if they are able to look out at green spaces
or even given a picture of nature to view.

We can learn from this relaxation technique and adopt a calmer
lifestyle. When seeking a breather from the hustle of daily living, copious
benefits exist when we carve out a place of our own to relax and observe
natural surroundings and life's passing.

I will sit in a quiet location for a short duration every day,
which can aid my overall well-being.

August 14

The best reason for having dreams is that in dreams no reasons are necessary.

—Ashleigh Brilliant

In sleep, our dreams may speak to us in ways our conscious brains cannot. Dreams shed light on our hopes and suppressed emotions. If we impede ideas and feelings during the day, they frequently surface at night—in the form of dreams. Some of these nocturnal thoughts seem to have no logic at all. They are only an interval for our brains to work out their intricate ideas and ramblings. These may appear as a movie we view where none of the characters are recognizable.

On the other hand, our dreams by day (which we control) can be happy times well spent. Artists and writers spend a great deal of time daydreaming—granting free reign to their imaginations while later relishing the reward of completed artworks and manuscripts.

Attending to the dream messages our subconscious whispers may unravel some of our more complex struggles. Keeping a journal at our bedside to record our creative and encouraging ideas can be a support to revisit whenever the mood strikes. Whether we are asleep or awake, dreaming is a remarkable variety of original thought at its best—a solace from an active-paced life we often live.

I will treasure when I have a dream of beauty
where I am an author, director, and star.

August 15

The greatest enemy of knowledge is not ignorance; it is
the illusion of knowledge.

—Stephen Hawking

There are several good books available that offer information about our
syndrome. Borrowing from a library or purchasing a book allows us to keep
abreast of the latest in research and development. Due to our symptom of
confusion, retaining new knowledge can be challenging, but it is possible
to learn with repetition, so let's be patient with ourselves.

Perhaps we have become well versed in our condition, opening
opportunities to speak at meetings, support groups, and schools.
Although we may discover knowledge daily (with the help of scientific
research available), most people who do not have fibromyalgia continue
to be unaware of its existence or the details of its symptoms. And the
misdiagnosing of patients continues. When we bring the recent findings
of our illness to others by way of a support group or conversation with
those who have been diagnosed, we can carry forward the message of hope.

I will search for opportunities
to broaden the understanding of my condition.

August 16

Time is a flowing river. Happy those who allow themselves
to be carried, unresisting with the current.
—Christopher Morley

We may hear people say, "Just go with the flow." Although this might be
a good suggestion, we admit at times that it can be easier said than done.
We possibly notice that those who do manage this laid-back lifestyle seem
more relaxed. The action of letting go and succumbing to the gentle glide
down the stream of life can be novel, unknown, and a little scary because
of change.

It takes courage to give in and be carried along, especially for those of
us who have always adhered to a routine or schedule. Going with the flow
requires a willingness to loosen structure, time, and perfection. Permitting
ourselves to play it by ear occasionally can lighten our perspective and lower
any pressing anxiety. What we get in return is calm, relaxed dispositions,
precisely what is necessary for our repeatedly stressed-out lives. We can
release our grip on selected aspects of our days, thereby creating space for
innovative and creative living.

I will flow with the tide of time today.

August 17

Remember, men need laughter sometimes more than food.
—Annie Fellows Johnston

We can benefit from the healing diversion amusement offers more than the average individual. Our lives can contain the weight of the necessities of dealing with our many symptoms. Tasks such as finding healthcare providers and medical and nutritional support to aid in coping can be time-consuming, costly, and genuine work. Without us realizing it, our days may become devoid of fun and laughter.

By perceiving the importance of laughter in our healing process, we can balance an element of chores and play—with an accent on amusing diversion. This balance can motivate us to continue to pursue opportunities for humor throughout our day.

It takes practice to notice opportunities to evoke laughter—relieving tension that can accompany chronic illness. Acquiring the knack of turning ordinary circumstances into opportunities for wit or downright silliness can help create a spirited mood, minimizing dull moments and turning them into utter folly.

I can indulge in my therapeutic sense of humor, and
my reward is laughter and fun.

August 18

True happiness is … to enjoy the present, without anxious
dependence upon the future.

—Lucius Annaeus Seneca

What a challenge we have when trying to live in the moment, particularly
if our moments are fraught with trying symptoms or repeated flare ups.
We regularly hope to open a door and discover happiness waiting for us.
Can we walk directly through to joy on the other side at will? We might
feel a key is necessary, and while anxiously hunting for that solution to
happiness, peace of mind and diminishing amounts of stress may seem
out of reach.

Our answer to accessing joy can easily be relaxation. When we are
relaxed, we exude a sunnier attitude. Let's try creating a little cheerfulness
today. It isn't complex. It can begin merely by us smiling and breathing
with ease. We can also discover delight in the mundane. Setting aside what
has been, and what will be, while finding joy in the now can help diminish
struggles. By accepting the moment, we acquire ease that flings wide any
door that ushers in happiness.

I will live in the present and experience true happiness.

August 19

Trust to hard work, perseverance, and determination. And the best motto for a long march is, "Don't grumble. Plug on."

—Sir Frederick Treves

We can witness the practice of not grumbling and plugging on at an outdoor walking track or trail. Where people of all ages engaged in some manner of exercise can be seen walking, running, skating, or cycling, no one seems to be complaining. They are getting somewhere and enjoying the great outdoors while doing so.

Surviving fibromyalgia is hard work. Our lives are expanded and bent by its presence. It can be difficult not to complain when fibro fog, fatigue, and pain are fighting for a position in our lives. The habit of journaling, spilling out all our woes and grumbles, can help us tolerate difficulties that few grasp and enable us to get on with this business of living.

Finding satisfaction within our daily routine and making notations in our journals can emphasize the possible, not the impossible. We unleash the expansion of well-being as we discern progress in acceptance of the encouraging in an often-dismaying condition.

I will travel the road of steadfast determination
with an emphasis on the beneficial.

August 20

I go to nature to be soothed and healed ...

　　　　　　　　　　　　　—John Burroughs

Chronic fatigue has slowed me considerably, and today, my walk among the everyday wonders that nature provides was at a snail's pace. On my pathway there, I was delighted by the antics of a bumblebee dipping in and out of morning glories and the serenade by a ubiquitous mockingbird. I paused by the banks of the Tennessee River and sank to a wooden bench. As I sat smiling beneath the delicate pink mimosa blossoms watching the lazy river roll by while the sun played peek-a-boo and a light breeze rustled the tulip poplar leaves, I breathed in the humid river air and felt healing commence.

When we recall the healing properties of nature, it is a surprise we don't all decide to pitch a tent under the stars until we entirely heal. With our schedules and commitments, we may habitually put our healing aside for the demands of everyday life. Nature's therapy can unclench those stiff muscles and offer respite from our pain, while we enjoy quality time basking in familiar yet somehow new vistas.

I will head outdoors today for a delightful
experience—healing with nature.

August 21

So often we dwell on the things that seem impossible rather than on the things that are possible. So often we are depressed by what remains to be done and forget to be thankful for all that has been done.

—Marian Wright Edelman

While observing any patterns of behavior, checking if we are in fact "dwelling on the impossible" alerts us to a need for reflection. If our moods fluctuate with another's action or inaction, we may perceive failure instead of possibilities. While maintaining the emphasis on *us*, we might notice a lessening of unnecessary strain, depression, and worries.

By concentrating on the potential in our lives, we provide ourselves with a mood boost, dispelling any depression. Keeping prominence on the doable helps minimize blue feelings and soothes any anxiety while making way for gratitude for our many accomplishments and abilities.

Frequently a change in scenery can pry us out of a rut as we welcome nature's new sights and sounds into our existence daily—if only for a few minutes. We can then face conflicts with a renewed emphasis on options and fresh eyes facilitated by the natural world. There will always be some degree of friction in our lives. Learning to turn away now and then is gratifying.

I will focus on possibilities,
reminding me of the value of gratitude in my life.

August 22

> Most of us, swimming against the tides of trouble the world knows nothing about, need only a bit of praise or encouragement—and we will make the goal.
>
> —Robert Collier

"Good job," "Keep it up," "Way to go" are all cheers heard from crowds propelling athletes in long-distance races, such as an Ironman competition. One would wonder what the attraction is. They seem so exhausted and miserable, but the likelihood of satisfaction of a job well done boosts their flagging spirits and carries them through. Some even get a burst of speed when they hear shouts of praise.

Would that we had our little crowd to clap and chant bright, encouraging phrases lifting us when we move about the day, whether one of meaningful work and projects or tedious, yet necessary, duties. Let's try attending an event showcasing the power of encouragement, whether it is a spelling bee, a race, or a gallery opening. Here we can witness people who may garner inspiration from others and leave with a paradigm of joy and sincerity. For as we encourage others, we come away motivated by a zeal that was perhaps not apparent—before we became a part of the cheer.

I will be one to praise or one to coast
or scramble to a spectacular finish.

August 23

We should have much peace if we would not busy ourselves
with the sayings and doings of others.

—Thomas a' Kempis

Valuable time might be wasted worrying about what friends, family, or
acquaintances may have pronounced—especially if it is *to* or *about* us. We
can consider the source and note if the criticism is valid. If it is untrue,
healthy distractions could benefit us, moving us into a state of calm and
relaxation. Here are some activities to bring our focus back to ourselves
and feeling confident about us:

- Make a list of our strengths and keep it in a location where we
  can view daily.
- Visit a library or bookstore and check out the latest bestsellers.
- Rearrange something as small as a spice rack or as large as a closet,
  creating a sense of accomplishment.

Our objective is to spend some alone time reconnecting with ourselves,
thereby building a healthier foundation for relationships. We break the
cycle of underscoring what is out of our control by stopping stress before
it becomes distress. As an alternative, we can choose to make our center
peace, choosing health over tension.

I choose peace.

August 24

Low self-esteem is like driving through life with your hand-break on.

—Maxwell Maltz

Life is a series of change. When it comes to adjustments, we have options to ponder while adapting to the new set of blueprints brought into our lives by chronic health issues. Releasing our (fatigue-based) brakes on life, we can approach new ventures while easing into healthy habits, such as moderately paced walking, especially outdoors. Electing to exit into the fresh air and benefit from light exercise may bring us the added benefit of meaningful contact with people, giving a boost to a possibly sinking self-esteem and loss of a sense of connection with others.

Chronic medical problems can be challenging, though by turning any downbeat feelings into valuable ones, we foster improvement. It is favorable to approach choices that will inflict change unhurriedly, allowing for comfort with our decisions. While coping with shifts in health using straightforwardness, we acquire confidence in ourselves and bolster our self-worth.

I will recall my strengths as I approach the changes in my life
with the hope of gliding through one more day.

August 25

Truth is always exciting. Speak it, then. Life is boring
without it.

—Pearl S. Buck

My mother held speaking the truth in high regard; consequently, as a child,
my harsh introduction into truth versus untruth made a lasting impression.
Later I understood it is not always wise to say everything that is on my
mind, even if I am being honest. I continue to adjust to this tempered-
down version of facts.

Having the integrity to be truthful about most aspects of our lives is
essential; honesty is a virtue to be treasured. However, being straightforward
about our medical problems to everyone we encounter may not always be
feasible. We might have one or two close, supportive people with whom
we share candidly, on occasion.

Revealing our chronic ailments to a healthy person can cause
discomfort on their part and possible regret on ours. In time we can learn
to respond with the socially acceptable, "I am fine" because we usually look
good (what a gift that is)! Putting a smile on our faces and going about the
day can help when we are struggling while reserving our health realities
for a support person.

I will speak my truth concerning my condition—when feasible.

August 26

I want to be able to live without a crowded calendar. I
want to be able to read a book without feeling guilty or
go to a concert when I like.

—Golda Meir

In our presymptomatic past, we might have attempted to be productive
every minute, scheduling a disproportionate amount of activities and
failing to say no. Prediagnosis may have found us spending an inordinate
amount of energy going from physician to physician, searching for the
why or wherefore of what ailed us. We may have never had a moment for
relaxation or repose and may have unwittingly increased our stress levels.
Primary care appointments, complete with lab tests and treatment plans,
are useful, and we can continue without them gaining the whole focus of
our day.

It is healthiest when we implement tension-releasing activities, such
as reading, playing a favorite game, marveling at the sunset, or frolicking
with a pet, as part of our wellness plan. By allotting a portion of every day
for worthwhile relaxing without guilt, we balance health issues with well-
being. Let's be kind to ourselves by not allowing anyone, especially us, to
deplete our enjoyment and personal interests.

I will enjoy life, for it is beneficial to my wellness.

August 27

Experience is a hard teacher because she gives the test first,
the lesson afterward.

—Vernon Law

Around and around we go, learning from our mistakes. Freedom to use either right or wrong judgment is the free will God gave us. Whether accurate or not, the fact that it is our own judgment is significant, for this is what makes it a learning experience. Usually, if another person tells us what to think and say or do, we might balk. We frequently learn life's lessons through our own decisions, by trial and error.

Perhaps we set out for a walk in the heat of a summer day, only to realize that the sun has zapped our energy. Ducking into the shade, we may surmise next time to wait for a decreased temperature to engage in active exercise. Or if sunlight and heat are overwhelming before we head out into the sunshine for an extended period, we can try a technique such as soaking a bandana in ice water, wringing out the excess water, and placing it around our necks, where it offers a cooling comfort. Learning through personal experiences may be all that we trust, although some individuals understand more quickly. Realizing we are achieving at precisely the correct pace is comforting.

I will accept my learning experiences,
knowing my path can lead to growth.

August 28

It only seems as if you are doing something when you're worrying.

—Lucy Maud Montgomery

It begins so casually; we start to think of a problem, perhaps not even detecting when thinking morphs into worry, initiating a perpetual cycle of anxiety. We could be experiencing this problematic symptom (anxiety) regularly. Identifying what triggers our upset can help release a portion of its detrimental effects. For some, it may be sensitivities to stimuli, such as bright lights, loud noises, and crowds. Still others might develop apparent unease around certain people or in specific situations. Several may be tense about their diagnosis and future health changes.

We can try various means for lessening tension when going out, such as carrying earplugs and water, keeping a spare set of keys, having sunglasses or a sun visor, limiting the duration of our outing, or avoiding crowds when we are overwhelmed. While standing in a line, if we are feeling hemmed-in, we can step to the side, giving ourselves space. By taking a few slow, calming breaths, we can reduce any apprehension. Also, through writing out our stressors, we can experience a release from our burdens and an advent of relaxation. We extract the worry out of stressful situations when we adopt a plan and preventive measures.

I can reduce my anxiety through awareness of my triggers.

August 29

There is no one giant step that does it. It's a lot of little steps.

—Peter A. Cohen

New Orleans's Lake Pontchartrain is well known for sudden bursts of squalls that can cause giant swells. As a young teenager, having had limited experience with these storms, I had no fear and thought the churning lake was fun! As a result of my adeptness at piloting our family's (home-built) cabin cruiser, my mother frequently called me to the wheel. This seemingly insignificant happening (steering over huge swells with ease) was a big confidence booster.

We can manage the little things, but there may be a stretch when even the so-called little things loom large. Stepping back and breathing deeply, we search for our inner strength to continue and experience success once more. Now and again, when tackling complications, we may fail to reach a specific goal—but we are not failures.

We can hold fast to our strengths, some of which have been developed by our ability to revel in small triumphs. Through relishing the lesser feats, we pave the way for our larger achievements. And as we encounter a new challenge, our ability to celebrate any victory can be of decided value.

I will accomplish something today, however small,
giving me a success and strengthening my self-confidence.

August 30

Birds sing after a storm; why shouldn't people feel as free
to delight in whatever remains to them?
—Rose Kennedy

When we concentrate on any disabilities that a life with a chronic illness diagnosis may bring, we invite negative feelings into our lives. Through releasing any losses and grasping enjoyments—paying attention to the fun—we are energized.

We can sing, dance (if only in our imaginations), laugh, meet new people, and embrace happiness. We could listen to the music we enjoy, humming or warbling along, make a recording of ourselves singing to our favorite melody. Let's take pleasure in our voices, which are their best when lifted in song and merry amusement.

Stroll outdoors (if only for a few minutes) and greet the sun, a great friend for the discouraged and fatigued. By shifting our focus from any disabilities and concentrating on our capabilities, we can keep depression and negativity at bay.

I will welcome fun into my life to help lighten my burden.

August 31

Get outside. Watch the sunrise. Watch the sunset ... Does
it make you feel big or tiny?

—Any Grant

Walking on the beach or near a natural body of water is one of my greatest
joys. I achieve a lot of my thinking while visiting the sand, the rock,
and the sea. Sometimes my thoughts drift into a daydream, and other
times they convert to praying. On most occasions during my walks, I am
gratefully in an enjoyable state that is devoid of any stressful thought.

It may appear at times that good health, pain-free days, and ease in
thinking are always out of reach. Just breathing in the fresh air can help
produce natural painkiller endorphins, aiding in cleaning out the cobwebs
of our fibro fog–addled brain. Although a sun-filled day can take credit
for elevating our moods, even being out on a cloudy day can do wonders
for our spirits, as nature is a first-rate mood stabilizer. Any cloud cover can
soothe our sensitive eyes while negating the use of sunglasses and wide-
brimmed hats.

While out and about in God's natural environment, we may find that
solutions to complications that eluded us before now may seem doable,
and we glean a fresh perspective and arrive back indoors with newfound
ideas and objectives to apply to our lives. Let's strive to visit Mother Nature
frequently and take in the pleasurable experience.

I will get outdoors and feel alive.

September 1

Pain is inevitable. Suffering is optional.
—Haruki Murakami

It might be easy to slip into the mire of self-pity, which at times can accompany our disorder, when we swiftly realize we are in a painful flare up. The choice is ours. We can either stumble along alone with our pain or call on spiritual guidance. Or we could be cruising along in a rare pocket of wellness—a welcoming remission. There may be periods when we are thriving at our best that we overlook the power of prayer, and relying on spiritual help is reserved for the trying stretches. Subsequently, stress may lumber or gallop in while we are not prepared, and being deficient of our usual arsenal of weapons (prayer), we go to battle unarmed. Have we not been down this road before?

Studies show that a faith-based person with chronic illness leads a happier, healthier life with less depression. Not neglecting our spiritual beliefs during challenging times or in periods of pain cessation and turning to God for help can be a healing comfort. Striving for and attaining an enriched life, even with a diagnosis of fibromyalgia, can be done, and yes, it is a lot of work at times, although having a firm foundation of faith is of immense benefit and a super coping tool.

I will choose spirituality over self-pity.

September 2

I used to go away for weeks in a state of confusion.
—Albert Einstein

It is a baffling symptom of fibromyalgia, this fibro fog. It can cause added stress (which only exacerbates our confusion), with frequent embarrassment and self-consciousness for some. After being frazzled by this symptom of mistakes and awkwardness, we may be surprised by the realization that periodically healthy people (normals) encounter mix-ups as well.

Using patience enables us not to expect perfect clarity in ourselves or others. The bewilderment that occurs in all people on occasion is an example of how we are alike. Not giving this symptom of confusion undue discouraging attention when it surfaces helps us sustain an upbeat attitude and smooths over mistakes that are sure to occur. It takes time to adapt to the frustration of fibro fog, but adaption can release some of the pressure we place on ourselves. It can be beneficial to accept these foibles with the realization that we are not the only ones who make errors, and our acceptance of confusion, wherever it exists, will help us endure with grace.

I adjust to my symptom of fibro fog
through noting my similarities to normals.

September 3

Our perfect companions never have fewer than four feet.
—Sidonie Gabrielle Colette

Pets can do exceedingly more than offering us companionship; they can additionally facilitate an increased level of serotonin, triggering an overall sense of well-being. Snuggling, or merely having a pet lie at our feet, can be a rewarding, healing experience for the chronically ill. Symptoms of depression could be supplanted with an atmosphere of contentment and love while lowering any elevated blood pressure that may exist.

Animals, including dog, cats, birds, reptiles, and so forth, are nonjudgmental companions, projecting an impression of comfort and trust. If you are unable to care for a pet, consider offering to walk a friend's dog now and again to experience the delight of a pet without the fatiguing, full-time responsibility. We can try pet sitting (if we are able), which can be a rewarding and fun experience.

Let's aim to arrange an outing to a petting zoo, a stable of horses, or a field of cows, sheep, or buffalo, and while we are there, we can sense the animal's calm spirit and be nurtured and rewarded with an abundance of goodwill. An outing like this can be beneficial alone, but the presence of children in this setting can render the encounter particularly worthwhile as we delight in their unbridled glee.

I will enjoy the experience of mutual comfort
by finding an animal to pet or cuddle.

September 4

If you could choose one characteristic that would get you through life, choose a sense of humor.

—Jennifer Jones

An awkward moment may occur if, when we are in conversation, an uncomfortable silence accompanied by tension takes over abruptly. The art of making such a situation humorous can be a skill worth acquiring. What a relief it is when someone utters a timely quip, replacing an uneasy lull within a conversation with a surge of laughter. Delightful laughing initiates a change in the environment in an instant and causes any nervousness to dissipate.

The saying, "Lighten up" can be used when we are beginning to feel anxiety or stress edging their way into our existence. How refreshing to realize we can alter our weighty personal loads that only escalate our symptoms. We can try replacing a stressful situation with a reason to smile, chuckle, or even giggle with abandon while reflecting on our glitches by applying a sense of humor and enjoying the rewards.

I will welcome a wealth of smiles and laughter into my day, altering my stresses into golden moments.

September 5

Creativity can be described as letting go of certainties.
—Gail Sheehy

In general most of us are conditioned to eat and sleep at specific times. For some, noon may suggest it is time for the second meal and six o'clock may signal the last meal of the day. As the sun sinks and the sky darkens each evening, it triggers the release of a natural hormone called melatonin, which causes sleepiness—usually.

Erratic eating schedules or lack of sleep affects the body's internal clock. We may not be adhering to any particular agenda and are listening to our inner clocks for direction. Freeing ourselves temporarily from constraints of society's preordained eating and sleeping schedules may lessen the tension and pressure.

Let's add a smidge of creativity to our lifestyles and stir it up a little by occasionally consuming traditional morning foods as the evening meal and enjoying breakfast at noon should we desire, or if we've had a restless, painful night. These actions can temporarily take the edge off rigid or anxiety-provoked agendas. When we implement a provisional flexible plan pending our routines getting back on track, we maintain our resourcefulness.

I will adopt a schedule today that is designed by me, for me.

September 6

If we couldn't laugh, we'd all go insane.

—Jimmy Buffet

Comedy may be lacking in our everyday lives that are crammed full of coming and going and thinking and doing or perhaps fatigue and stagnation. What is our reason for not practicing one of the most natural health-conscious methods daily—laughter? Perchance we might feel conceivably too depressed to laugh. There appears to be scientific proof of the ability of laughter to heal.

If we are currently depressed, one way to slide into gaiety is to start from our present mood. We can watch a drama on television and have an emotionally cleansing cry. Releasing our repressed feelings provides a welcome feeling relief. Now we may be ready for something sunnier. Next, let's try a book or movie with a mixture of drama and comedy—dramedy. By this time, we could be craving a comedy and can relish the entertainment it will provide. When we expose ourselves to wit and engage in laughter, there is a boost in natural pain-relieving endorphins and an ease in aches and troubles as our muscles mellow in the interim.

I possess all the essential ingredients for a recipe of wellness;
mix in a little unwinding until it forms peaks of laughter.

September 7

Do not anticipate trouble or worry about what may never
happen. Keep in the sunlight.

—Benjamin Franklin

There is a tendency for everyone, at some time or another, to fret and
worry. It seems as if when we dismiss one apprehension, another takes its
place. Troubling thoughts seem to build one on another like a carelessly
placed Jenga piece, threatening to bring everything crashing down.

A useful coping tool can be to fashion a worry box or God box, a
simple solution to overwhelming distress capable of bestowing satisfying
results. Find or make a small container by using cardboard, wood, ceramic,
etc. In the absence of these materials, a simple envelope will do. When we
begin to fret, we can write our concern/fear on a small piece of paper along
with any requests we want to turn over to God and place in our worry box.

Next, we simply forget about it. That's correct—we do not give it
another thought. When the next worrying thought comes along, we apply
the same principle. Before long, we may notice a decrease in our stewing
over troubles. By implementing this system as a means of releasing our
burdens, we have an opportunity to lay tension aside and turn instead to
brighter thoughts.

I will embrace sunnier thoughts by releasing my worries into a God box.

September 8

Keep it simple.

—Alfred Eisenstaedt

In an average day, many decisions are necessary to keep our lives flowing effortlessly. To prevent stress from accelerating out of control, a certain amount of planning is advantageous. Trying to maintain a balance between overscheduling and becoming inactive is a challenge.

We could question our priorities. Are we cleaning frequently and organizing relentlessly? Perhaps keeping busy to occupy our thoughts with activities other than our health challenges is a form of coping. A healthful, healing accomplishment might be a day when we include responsibilities *and* recreation. If we allow our household belongings to accumulate in plain sight and only clear the clutter when visitors are coming, we can consider downsizing by donating or passing on heirlooms and possessions. With this gesture, we make room in our lives for simplicity to flourish.

I will plan for simplicity, a boost to my well-being, and contentment.

September 9

Fill what's empty, empty what's full, and scratch where
it itches.

—Wallis Simpson, duchess of Windsor

What an incredible sense of freedom when we relinquish any unnecessary
restrictions. For example, the burden of a crowded schedule could be
augmenting our stress. Let's try emptying it and have lunch with a friend
instead or merely delighting in an occasional day off. Paring back routines
to fit our present abilities can result in a more manageable way of life.

Perhaps we lack exercise (which can contribute to increased fatigue and
pain), or maybe we suffer from the opposite, where we may exceed our
activity threshold, resulting in flare ups. As we carve out space for gentle
daily exercise, we can begin to observe the significant benefits: less fatigue
and pain, increased muscle toning, and weight management.

When we are first confronted with realities of day-to-day living with
a chronic medical condition, we may become overwhelmed by the loss
of our former skills. Compiling a list of our agendas or routines brings
clarity to what necessitates attention and where we might scale back. By
appreciating that a healthful modification in lifestyle is valuable, we can
promote our welfare.

I will formulate an adjustment where necessary
in my current lifestyle.

September 10

I have not failed ten thousand times. I have successfully
found ten thousand ways that do not work.
                                        —Thomas Edison

Since we are all different creatures, it is hardly possible to light on one plan
that suits all, as this is frequently a trial-and-error and time-consuming
ordeal. However, if we organize a record of any treatments, supplements, or
alternative methods we have tried to date, we will find it easy to track what
works and what doesn't while keeping a record of all we have benefited
from, even in minute ways. As we discover something that brings about the
desired effect, we can cross it off our list, giving space for new information.
Perhaps we check out a new herbal remedy that we hear has helped others,
only to have it cause indigestion or other disagreeable side effects. It would
be beneficial to include notes about any treatments with unsatisfactory
results as well.

With the confusion we regularly face, having a helpful versus
unhelpful inventory can help if we are asked by a physician or friend,
"What treatments have you attempted to date?" We can maintain an
encouraging attitude while persisting in our efforts, for our assumption
may be that we will remember these details, though often we do not.

I will be receptive to the successes I encounter
and learn from any letdowns.

September 11

We don't even know how strong we are until we are forced
to bring that hidden strength forward. In times of tragedy,
of war, of necessity, people do amazing things. The human
capacity for survival and renewal is awesome.

—Isabel Allende

The unexpected has a way of shaking our universe, of challenging what is
real. But life will return to normal in time, and changes, whether negative
or positive, will always be a part of everyone's reality. Although we feel
we may never forget a memorable catastrophic event, in time there is a
softening, an easing of pain, and we can glance back without full anguish.
Know that we are not alone with feelings of outrage against tragic events,
be they pandemic, flood, hurricane, or terrorist, we all join in memory and
reflection as we pray for a stronger, gentler tomorrow.

There could be personal tragedies in our past that may haunt us. We
can take the opportunity to do the grieving and mourn for what may be
lost, which can precipitate healing and growth. Minor misfortune can at
times appear threatening, but it is merely one of the many occurrences
and opportunities for growth that transpire in everyone's life to varying
degrees.

Renewal will replace suffering
as strength becomes my anthem.

September 12

Accept your defeats
With your head up and your eyes open
With the grace of a woman or a man,
Not the grief of a child ...

—Kara DiGiovanna

The difficulties of living with a diminished health capacity may threaten to overwhelm us if we dwell on any defeat. Perhaps we longed to enjoy a bicycle ride or take a small hike, only to find ourselves dizzy, breathless— unable to endure. Even a walk or a conversation may require shortening because of fatigue, pain, or other symptoms. We may come to realize that overdoing activities or exercise leaves us more vulnerable to pain, stress, and injury.

By setting smaller goals and working slowly toward more challenging physical endeavors, we ensure the chance of a successful outcome. Keeping the focus on what we *can* achieve while knowing we may have an improved day tomorrow can maintain a minimum of hassle while enhancing our natural calm and grace. And as we accept life's ups and downs, our attention toward successes is enabled.

I will recognize my limits while focusing on my abilities.

September 13

Every man can transform the world from one of monotony
and drabness to one of excitement and adventure.
                                        —Irving Wallace

I delayed taking a walk and didn't arrive outdoors until the afternoon and
headed into the unusually mild air. Raindrops began to make their way to
the ground lazily, and it would have been easy to return inside. I ventured
on, and the rain picked up as I encountered a woman walking her two dogs,
an Irish wolfhound and a rescue dog. We eyed the approaching clouds—
weighty with moisture—but continued chatting as we strolled. I enjoyed
sharing my walk with a new acquaintance and her canine companions,
turning my stroll in a late summer rain shower into a mini adventure.

Every new day arrives unique and different. This awareness can result
in specifically pondering how to spend this precious time. Who knows—
instead of monotony, we could welcome the possible arrival of excitement
and adventure, however elusive they may be. It might not be what we
planned, but every now and again, it keeps life fresh and exciting when
we achieve the unexpected, respond spontaneously, and experience a bit
of adventure.

I will greet each new day by wondering what pure excitement
I can transform into my today.

September 14

I've learned that you can make a mistake and the world doesn't end.

—Lisa Kudrow

Extra pressure could be exerted on us prediagnosis if we frequently sought to do things just so, avoiding mistakes at all costs. Any inclination to always be correct will not ensure happiness and could add additional tension, cranking up our nervous systems. If we find ourselves caught up in perfectionism, we can adopt a gentler approach, seeking a more balanced life that allows for a few blunders now and again. This softer slant on life can begin easing anxious feelings.

Our lives can then unfold organically, without trying to manage every detail, and this action might usher in ease of living when we accept that mistakes *do* transpire. What's the worst that can happen? By acknowledging that thinking of the worst scenario and the unlikelihood that it will happen, we help to gain some perspective on a problem and dial down anxiety levels. When mistakes occur—and they will—we can recognize them as part of any regular living process.

Today I will allow myself the right to be human.

September 15

I have no regrets. I wouldn't have lived my life the way I did if I was going to worry about what people were going to say.

—Ingrid Bergman

There is something to be said for those who choose to be themselves, whether accepted by all, or a handful. We each have the choice of living a worthwhile life with no regrets, comprising the taking of chances and encountering the risks that accompany growth.

The possibility that there could be people who speak unkind or unsettling words toward us exists, and not agonizing over such incidents is a constructive approach. It is our handling of adversity that determines the level of self-confidence we possess.

Attempting to please everyone is impossible and can be detrimental, as people-pleasing could lead to further stress issues, creating additional burdens and disquiet in our already symptom-laden existences. But merely doing our best, trying not to step on too many toes along the way, is a useful plan. When we keep active with hobbies or pleasurable tasks, we can reduce the quantity of energy spent worrying and fretting, thereby increasing the flow of valuable and encouraging thoughts.

I live one day at a time with its ups and downs,
moving forward without regrets.

September 16

For fast-acting relief, try slowing down.

—Lily Tomlin

Life can move us along breathlessly, and some of the consequences of finding ourselves overwhelmed can be a flare up of symptoms. Even when we are fatigued, we may repeatedly be endeavoring to go a bit faster in attempts to catch up. We might deny ourselves permission to slow down, feeling we must work harder to maintain the pace, which then magnifies pressure. But whose speed are we attempting to shadow? Noting that becoming overwhelmed can set us back even further, we can try not to overdo.

Learning to prioritize schedules can lighten our load, allowing the opportunity for relaxation. We can begin varied activities, such as gentle walking, bird watching, meditation, or sitting by a body of water or fountain, which are all beneficial for balanced immune systems. Allotting a portion of each day for health-boosting activities can be enjoyable as well as a pressure-releasing mechanism. By adopting a manner of ease when approaching our daily schedules, our symptoms become more manageable, and we can delight in pleasurable activities.

I will relax my pace today,
knowing I am helping my wellness.

September 17

Every now and again take a good look at something not made with hands, a mountain, a star, the turn of a stream. There will come to you wisdom and patience and solace and, above all, the assurance that you are not alone in the world.

—Sidney Lovett

We have the gift of such abundant beauty in our natural surroundings designed by our Creator. While struggling with the many symptoms of chronic medical problems, we may lose sight of these numerous treasures that reside in the great outdoors.

We could try putting out bird feeders or hummingbird stations and enjoying watching the various entertaining feathered friends even if all we have is a small porch with no green space. Not all of us have the abilities or the grounds to plant a large garden, but a container of flowers is usually within our capabilities, and the hummingbirds it may attract can generate healing smiles.

While we unwind outdoors by a stream or perhaps a flowering shrub, we may be greeted by butterflies navigating a loopy pattern. Through opening our eyes and acknowledging nature, we can initiate an appreciation of Mother Nature's fantastic gifts and the beauty bestowed around us. As we emerge from our burden-riddled lives, enjoying the marvels of terra firma, we free our spirits to soar.

The beauty of God's gifts vanquishes my self-pity
and rejuvenates my peacefulness.

September 18

I wish they would only take me as I am.
—Vincent Van Gogh

But who are we now? Do we remain as close with a certain few people as before our illness arrived on the scene, or have differences occurred in multiple subtle and not-so-subtle ways? It seems impossible to manage the fallout that comes with a medical dilemma without significant change. Even our families may have trouble adjusting to fluctuating shifts in our circumstance, which could leave them at times bereft for words of encouragement or understanding.

Helping those we care about to take us as we *are*, not as we were, can be an exercise in mutual acceptance. We are flawed creatures, as is everyone, with many attributes and possibilities that are ripe to be revealed. Our own recognition of our medical issues and the effects on our bodies and minds can ease the way for those we work and play with to perceive us and treat us with the support and understanding we so desire.

I am still me;
fibromyalgia can never take that away.

September 19

One can find so many pains when the rain is falling.
—John Steinbeck

How many of us feel the ravages of changing weather upon our bodies? For several, the first sign of a shift in the elements may be increased fibro fog. Intensification in pain levels could result from atmospheric pressure changes, particularly a drop in pressure. Looking ahead when we are planning outings or appointments by checking the conditions outdoors can be the difference between an enjoyable excursion or taxing ourselves and causing unnecessary discomfort.

We can become as comfortable as possible when a low-pressure weather system passes through our area, softening its impact on us. Let's put together a comfort kit containing heating pads, favorite blankets, pillows, and stuffed animals. We should also have Epsom salts and a muscle relief topical ointment on hand, all to assist our wellness. Brew up a pot of calming herbal tea and hunker down with a good book and soft music until the storm has moved on. Or engage in some gentle relaxation stretches.

With stormy conditions, there can be spectacular sunsets or rainbows. When we step outdoors (or view them through a window), we admire their aerial beauty, and in our awe of nature's magnificence, our pain may lessen.

I will search for the rainbow
that can be a lovely distraction from pain.

September 20

Every path has its puddle.

—English proverb

We have had moments when we wished for good health or at a minimum had a syndrome without "chronic" attached to the description. We might even have bemoaned that some illnesses receive a wealth of research and attention while our condition is relatively disregarded by the medical community, research, and the general public, due to its complexity. The reality that it can be misunderstood and misdiagnosed can cause us significant frustration, although continuing to dwell on such thoughts may bring on a bout of self-pity.

Realistically, though, all people have their share of dilemmas. By acknowledging this, we can highlight our achievements and not our deficiencies. Perhaps we could purchase items from one of the organizations that contributes a percentage of its benefits to fibromyalgia research, thereby helping our cause with each purchase. Occasionally we might yearn for the time before we developed health problems or for fewer hurdles, but on a good day, we can turn mere survival into gratification and contentment.

With an improved attitude,
I can obtain a healthier pattern of living.

September 21

A good garden may have some weeds.

—Thomas Fuller

Gardening is such a rewarding activity; even indoor plant life has therapeutic benefits. Those of us who delight in the growing of—be it herbs, flowers, or vegetation—usually acknowledge the beauty of our handiwork by emphasizing the blossoms or fruit, not the stray weeds. And so it is with health problems as well. When we put a greater emphasis on our progress, not our setbacks, we thrive.

We endeavor for renewed abilities and a cessation of pain by not allowing the unhelpful to dictate to us during a problematic interval. And through this attitude, we can achieve great strides in well-being. Turning our attention to the bounty in our lives can lighten burdens, bringing relaxation to those tight muscles. And by tolerating a degree of the unkempt in our otherwise pleasant existence, we foster emotional growth. Every garden has weeds, every summer has clouds, and every life has frustrating moments.

I will concede to weeds (symptoms) in my life
but will not let them control my day.

September 22

My disease is one of the best things that have happened to me; it has pulled me out of a quietly desperate life toward one full of love and hope.

—Tom O'Connor

Many chronic illness patients may hesitate to consider any positive aspects of medical dilemmas, although health problems have a way of waking us to hopeful areas in our lives that may have previously gone undetected. Walking, talking, and remembering prediagnosis were a given. There can be a modification of all aspects of our lives, however, and we may gaze longingly on what we once took for granted.

Instead of wishing things were better, more than, or less than, we can foster progress with awareness and acceptance. Swinging wide the doorway to hope, we may commence with the unfolding of a more relaxed and renewed love of life. Gone is the desperation that might have appeared to shadow, us and in its stead lies renewed courage to face what is—and make it excellent.

I will reflect on my transformed life
and value the changes that have ensued.

September 23

We do not believe in ourselves until someone reveals that
deep inside us something is valuable, worth listening to,
worthy of our trust, sacred to our touch.
Once we believe in ourselves, we can risk curiosity,
wonder, spontaneous delight or any experience that reveals
the human spirit.

—E. E. Cummings

It is in the character of humans to look for validation from others: friends,
family, or anyone who echoes our sense of values. It is not our adversities
that define us but how we think and exist—despite them.

We may have already discovered God to be the one who reveals
our real worth. His gift of belief can disclose aspects of us that we had
not previously apprehended, and the freedom of empowerment we will
experience is akin to opening new windows to the soul.

There is an ease that comes from established self-worth as we attempt
new endeavors, without permitting health obstacles to hinder further
growth. Now let us engage with the curious eyes of a child the pure wonder
and delight in every season God has created as we also bring to light the
beauty and character of our own and others' human spirits.

I will believe in myself and garner the rewards.

September 24

Hope, the best comfort of our imperfect condition.

—Edward Gibbon

Having fibromyalgia can drain us to the core. When it is coupled with the many debilitating symptoms that appear endless with seemingly no relief in sight, we may ask how to achieve comfort from the many perplexities that accompany our medical condition.

Hope gives us something to adhere to, something to strive for when we are worn thin and our souls are wailing from our pain. In light of the disappointment that despite ongoing fibromyalgia research, there are no new revelations, hope can be a solace.

Now and again, as we focus on something other than the negativities of our chronic illness, we leave the door open for belief in positive feelings (hope). With the assurance that there is more to our lives than fibromyalgia, we rise up.

I have an infliction of an imperfect condition;
nevertheless, I am deeply comforted by hope.

September 25

What I dream of is an art of balance, of purity and
serenity devoid of troubling or depressing subject matter, a
soothing, calming influence on the mind, something like
a good armchair which provides relaxation from physical
fatigue.

—Henri Matisse

A certain amount of trouble is to be expected in everyone's daily lives,
although we experience different hurdles from our counterparts. Depression
is one of our various symptoms, and it takes an effort to fight off the blues.
We may feel it is simpler to pull the covers over our heads when trouble
visits, although the aftermath of excessively resting can be tight, painful
muscles, increasing fatigue, depression, and guilt.

A plethora of disheartening moments can tip our scales to the negative
if we are overexerting ourselves physically. Having fatigue as a daily
symptom and attempting to push past it to exhaustion invites a flare
up of symptoms. As we offset moderate exercise with relaxation, we can
welcome stress reduction and encourage wellness. When an opening in our
schedules for soothing, calming influences is set aside, serenity not only
becomes a possibility; it is a reality.

Today I will be unruffled.

September 26

Dedicate yourself to the good you deserve and desire for yourself. Give yourself peace of mind. You deserve to be happy. You deserve delight.

—Hannah Arendt

Tonight I once again admire the blessing of a breathtaking color display at dusk. As I walk toward the vivid orange of the setting sun—a glowing intensity—I smile with delight. When I observe the splendor of nature's light show, I pause and remember my gratitude for these simple treasures just waiting for discovery. And I acknowledge that being in nature eases the most challenging of my days, taking the weight out of difficulties and leaving joy in its stead.

Years of flagging self-esteem that can accompany chronic medical problems may leave us periodically doubting our self-worth and the ability to enjoy life. It is often an exhausting struggle to maintain dignity in the face of adversity. We know that peace can reign within our hearts and minds and the happiness and appreciation of beauty we encounter could have lasting restorative value. This knowledge can brighten the most troubling of situations.

I will acknowledge serenity, happiness, and delight in my life.

September 27

Relaxation means releasing all concern and tension and letting the natural order of life flow through one's being.
—Donald Curtis

Being adept at relaxation is advantageous, as our natural posture might be wary, and we may have adopted a fight-or-flight response. Recognizing when we do clench our muscles might be the first step of softening them. Focusing on any discomfort can intensify pain's impact by keeping our bodies overly taut and aching. The knowledge that we could achieve relief from tension is reassuring.

Let's try this exercise: Find a quiet place and recline on a firm surface (a bed or recliner will do), and if we are on the floor, tuck a rolled towel under our necks to slightly raise our heads. Rest in this position for approximately ten minutes; our brains may continue processing our troubles initially. Within a few minutes, we may perceive fewer tense concerns occupying our thoughts, and we may experience a clear sense of flowing along the peaceful river of life.

I will relax my body and mind today
as a healthy means of coping with tension.

September 28

There is no despair so absolute as that which comes with
the first moments of our first great sorrow, when we have
not yet known what it is to have suffered and be healed,
to have despaired and have recovered hope.

—George Eliot

Sorrow is an inevitable part of everyone's life. Whether it is a loss of a
cherished pet or receiving a bad health diagnosis, grief is an enormous
challenge. Despair and doubt can envelop us, settling about us like a
weighty cloak. This dismal condition can linger until we display the
initiative of traversing beyond it.

It is through a generous attitude and spirit that we often attain notable
relief from any hopelessness. Comfort befalls us through compassion
toward others and ourselves as we consider those outside ourselves. When
we reach out in friendship to people and assist them (when able), we
generate benefits for all. Giving of ourselves can precipitate healing and a
healthier mind-set to our—from time to time—miserable condition.

I will be considerate of others,
discovering my despair diminished and solace with hope.

September 29

Friendship improves happiness and abates misery, by the
doubling of our joy and the dividing of your grief.
—Marcius Tullius Cicero

Fatigue, pain, and irritability are some of the symptoms and difficulties of
our condition. There may be days when we are grateful when we feel loved
despite our many fluctuating struggles and attitudes due to our symptoms.
All it takes (in some cases) is a lack of sleep or being overwhelmed to tip
us into problematic territory. Some knew us before we became ill and have
stuck around regardless of our many hurdles while others who are new in
our lives may not comprehend our shifting moods due to our symptoms.

And while we may care for family or friends, we can remind ourselves
that love functions best when we are not expecting perfection in ourselves
or others. We can be thankful for those who have stood by us through
our diagnosis with the varying shifts that go with relationships with the
chronically ill.

Let's try to let go of the unrealistic requirements of our moods by
accepting what is—while managing a smile on a rough day. Knowing the
day may be tough on those around us as well keeps happiness close at hand.

I know I can love and be loved.

September 30

Separate we come, and separate we go, and this be it
known, is all that we know.
—Conrad Aiken

A portion of us may feel alone from time to time. This may bring about
feelings of loneliness and isolation. Try visiting a flower shop for a
comforting place with a useful illustration of being separate yet content. We
can admire single-stem flowers bursting with color, some with fragrance
so intoxicating, each standing stark, beautiful, and graceful. Their sole
design causes our enjoyment.

It is possible to be unaccompanied yet devoid of any feelings of solitude
by focusing on the advantages, not disadvantages, of going solo. The
knowledge that we can carve out our agendas without checking with
another is certainly a bonus.

We can turn our alone time into a time of comfort and relaxation.
Let's experience sitting in a comfortable chair for a brief period, breathing
slowly and evenly, and detecting the sense of calm that can settle in when
nothing feels forced. Gazing out a window and observing people strolling
by provides a connection with others even when we are by ourselves. And
similar to the single blossom, we too can stand whole and beautiful.

I need not fear solitude.

October 1

Sometimes I go about pitying myself, and all the time I
am being carried on great winds across the sky.
　　　　　　　　　—Ojibway Dream Song

Walking in nature alone, whether in woods or valley, is a much-loved activity of mine. When I am alone, the solitude enhances the beauty of the pure magnificence of my landscape. There are occasions when I feel drawn to the outdoors because of feeling out of sorts or down. I recognize a stroll in green spaces will relieve my doldrums, and Mother Nature never fails me.

Not succumbing to self-pity can be a challenge if we spend a significant amount of our day alone (especially cooped up indoors). Encounters with green spaces can be just what we need, easing us from the clutches of self-absorption and back into acknowledging our world of incredible abundance and beauty.

While we are out reveling in the natural world, we may peruse our surroundings and detect subtle things, such as a gentle breeze, humidity, or dryness or perhaps hearing or sighting various birds. Next we might obverse the trees and at which stage they are in their leaf cycle. When looking to the sky, we can view color or a lack thereof and clouds or open air, calm or windy. After an interval, we may detect that our former sinking mood has lifted, and we are merely right here, discerning wonderment in the humblest sightings in our environment.

I journey to nature to keep myself free of self-pity.

October 2

Take your work seriously, but never yourself.
                                —Dame Margot Fonteyn

A significant number of fibromyalgia patients are former type-A personalities, so taking our work seriously is rarely a stretch. It is in loosening up where we may struggle. If a no-nonsense disposition extends beyond our occupation and seems to dominate our self-perception, we could consider options for easing up. Viewing ourselves with a more relaxed eye and searching for a bit of humor in our challenging situation is a valuable objective.

One technique to tone down an overly solemn manner is to smile regularly; this may lead to a more lighthearted, possibly playful disposition. When we adopt a carefree approach—whenever or wherever possible—we exude a pleasant temperament whether we are alone or with others. Let's practice being mellow and experience life to the fullest, where we may reach a point of balance, taking a softer, more blissful look at ourselves.

Today I will remember to add a little playfulness
to my frequently dull life.

October 3

When you hold resentment toward another, you are bound to that person or condition by an emotional link that is stronger than steel. Forgiveness is the only way to dissolve that link and get free.

—Catherine Ponder

We can be comforted when we realize that once we have forgiven, it is out of our hands. Some relationships may remain intact when we exercise forgiveness, while it may be best to terminate others because of critical unresolvable issues. The choice to proceed unencumbered by a toxic relationship can be wise.

Anger or other undesirable emotions, which shepherd in resentment, can wreak havoc on our bodies and minds, and we might clench our teeth unaware, causing painful TMJ syndrome to develop. Further tightening of the muscles in the shoulders and neck can lead to increased back and neck pain. And the list goes on for all the physical ill effects resentment can initiate.

To benefit from forgiveness fully, we fare best by not revisiting anyone's off-putting behaviors. We hear forgiveness is for the forgiver. Its purpose is to reduce and eliminate anger or resentment and transport us to a place of peace. By letting go of someone's hurtful behaviors, we can vanquish feelings of ire or bitterness toward another as we welcome peace in its stead.

I can forgive today,
embracing the serene freedom that transpires.

October 4

Thy fate is the common fate of all,
Into each life some rain must fall,
Some days must be dark and dreary.
                    —Henry Wadsworth Longfellow

We may wake slowly on certain days, perhaps due to a low-pressure system in our vicinity. Our bodies thrash about, clenched with a painful cramped muscle. As we seek an increase in rest, we urge ourselves to return to deep slumber, where pain does not reside. Too late! Our minds are awake, focusing on the nagging spasm in our bodies. On mornings such as these, we may move slower and be generally depressed throughout the day. Remaining in a dark and dreary mood can adversely affect our stress and pain levels.

If depression continues for more than two weeks, we can consider scheduling an appointment with a physician to rule out thyroid disease or clinical depression. Both can be managed with medication. By getting to the foundation of our melancholy, we cease to stew in this miserable state for an extended time. If we are experiencing a blue mood, we know that it will improve soon and that brighter days are ahead.

I can face my rain-soaked days and greet them
with an umbrella of hope in hand—knowing I have options.

October 5

Don't let the noise of others' opinions drown out your own inner voice.

— Steve Jobs

There will always be people whose opinions differ from ours. But by maintaining a positive inner voice, we leave less room for negativity from others. The skills we tell ourselves we can or cannot achieve can have a profound effect on us, and our self-chatter can be affirmative and healing or detrimental and self-defeating. The following are examples of positive self-talk: I am a child of God; I am a beautiful person; I deserve healing; and I believe in me.

Occasionally we may struggle with the concept of optimism in the face of reduced health and wellness. We can create a space for the favorable to happen in our lives by steering clear of life's disappointments. And there can be a lessening of any adversarial effects of chronic illness through the practice of surrounding ourselves with encouraging, supportive people. We are not our condition; we are something greater, and we can remain hopeful while striving for wellness.

I will put out my welcome mat for hopeful optimism.

October 6

Patience can't be acquired overnight. It is just like building
up a muscle. Every day you need to work on it.
　　　　　　　　　　　　　　　—Eknath Easwaran

We may occasionally take for granted those who are nearest and dearest.
Why might we sometimes treat those we care about the most with less
concern than total strangers? Friendships of the chronically ill can be
tested, requiring our tolerance and understanding. We might ponder how
relationships flourish and how they crumble. What makes them work may
appear an enigma. And we can remain patient with ourselves if we are
ending or redefining a bond as emotions could fluctuate with any change.

　　Most would agree that it takes work to maintain any connection, and
doing our part of being tolerant when dealing with others can assist in
the flourishing of both friendships and love. When we acknowledge that
patience is valuable to any thriving relationship, progress is exhibited. As
we apply this practical approach to relations as a whole, they can begin to
prosper with a sense of peace and harmony.

Today I will exercise patience
while interacting with friends and family.

October 7

In the life of each of us, I said to myself, there is a place remote and islanded, and given to endless regret or secret happiness.

—Sarah Orne Jewett

While we experience a gamut of emotions throughout our lives, some appear to stick around. Others may drift away. And because of these feelings, we take away memories that linger with us and can turn us into serene spirits or perhaps even bitter individuals. If we hang onto regrets, we might feel justified in listing our every qualm, spiraling into dissatisfaction or dissolving into hopelessness.

When we collect every precious memory and add new ones at will, we provide a cushion to lean upon when weary. Visiting loved ones in person or reconnecting through a photograph is one approach to build upon our happiness. The recording of real events and dreams that evoke a smile compensates us with something uplifting while seizing our attention during possible trying interludes. If past regrets seem to be bogging us down, we can try to go to the Lord in prayer and ask for his tender mercies to once again restore happiness.

I will bring my happiness into the sunlight.

October 8

When a person is down in the world, an ounce of help is better than a pound of preaching.
—Edward Bulwer-Lytton

The telephone is a useful tool to keep in touch and convey that we care about our friends who have fibromyalgia. Often those of us with a chronic medical condition welcome someone who is willing to listen. Many misunderstand our syndrome, and we might feel alone as a result. This isolation could be detrimental if it leads to lasting depression.

There might be circumstances when a fellow chronically ill individual approaches us with a problem, and we offer support. However, when a person is encountering significant issues, referral to professional guidance may be the most beneficial. Our responsibility as a pal is to help but not pressure. We can include the person's name in our prayer list. Another option is to accompany them outdoors to sit or engage in a leisurely walk. This can often bring a fresh perspective to problems that seem to dominate. By sharing our experiences, exchanging information, and assisting where we can, everyone benefits.

I will offer a hand of friendship
to a fibromyalgia patient.

October 9

There is a definite process by which one made people into friends, and it involves talking to them and listening to them for hours at a time.

—Rebecca West

Life-altering changes following a health diagnosis can affect many a friendship. Having diminished capabilities can strain relationships, especially those with individuals who knew us when we were healthy, busy achievers. The time and effort that goes into friendship can be taxing, causing us to feel overwhelmed when we interact with others. Subsequently, the strain on our bodies and minds that comes with prolonged health challenges can make it problematic to continue relationships in our usual patterns.

Prediagnosis, visiting with friends was a natural occurrence, and we could easily spend hours in the company of a good companion. Postdiagnosis, activities and events that were previously enjoyable or even amusing can often become a hardship.

We foster a more comfortable transition when we come to understand how and when to discuss our limitations and how to pace ourselves when we are in the presence of others. Achieving a balance between withdrawal from society and the overload of personal contacts is a healthy and valuable choice.

I have a new regard for my requirements
as they pertain to my relationships.

October 10

The whole life of man is but a point of time; let us enjoy it.
—Plutarch

Do we feel an urge to know the particular time at all hours? This habit can heap more urgency onto an already challenging day. Clockwatching when we are in pain or discomfort seems to prolong our misery. A prudent decision could be to limit the number of clocks in our environment. By adapting to a more flexible schedule, we can lower stress factors rather than tightly adhering to the hour. On a day with an appointment, we can set a timer indicating when to leave, rendering glancing at the time unnecessary, helping to lessen our anxiety.

Studies reveal that checking the time during the night is sleep disruptive. It seems the more we watch the clock, the more awake we become, setting the stage for insomnia. For enhanced sleep and decreased pain, we can overcome an urge to look at the hour by facing any clock away from us when we retire. This will help us return to blissful slumber in preparation for a day with tension reduction, teeming with moments to relish.

I will resist my curiosity to know the hour; instead,
I will relax and enjoy my every moment.

October 11

There are two ways of meeting difficulties: you alter the difficulties or you alter yourself meeting them.
—Phyllis Bottome

How we approach our challenges says a great deal about who we are. Some may be in a depression of sorts that could lead to isolation or remaining in bed or the couch much of the day, with health issues becoming the main theme of their lives. Many of us (perhaps in denial) continue as if everything was the same. While this appears to be useful, repeatedly overdoing it requires expanded recovery time. There may be others who exhaust themselves devoting most of their energy to searching for permanent healing for their condition. Somewhere in between, there is a balance of acceptance of our limitations—without giving up.

When we are in a flare up, we can mark our calendars, noting the date the increase in symptoms began, what the symptoms were, and what precipitated the flare up, be it physical or emotional (or both). Then, by noting what relieves the flare up and recording the specifics, the event can be released from our thoughts, freeing up room for enjoyment. It may be challenging to remain upbeat during frustrating symptoms. However, by scheduling recuperation time along with acceptance and having a coping strategy, we can conquer hurdles with an improved tactic.

My fibromyalgia is a fact,
but I can alter my coping method.

October 12

(Sleep is) the golden chain that ties health and our bodies together.

—Thomas Dekker

For the majority, a day crammed with activity brings a night of welcomed, stress-free sleep. However, if we max out our activities, we might not hit the sheets and fall instantly to a much-needed rest. Overdoing it can leave us struggling to relax into slumber. Light exercise during our day has been proven to be optimal and can help us fall asleep quicker, with fewer nocturnal awakenings.

Engaging in calming pursuits late in the day and into the evening can assist in ensuring our chances of a restful night. For ideal sleep, it is recommended that we abstain from exercise and eating within three hours of bedtime. By dimming the lights and lowering the volume (if we are listening to music in our homes) at dusk and reading a boring book before bed, we can often lull ourselves to sleep. These actions send a message to the body, which triggers the release of a naturally occurring hormone called melatonin, which relaxes us further and gets us ready for refreshing sleep.

I will look upon sleep as the healing tool it is,
nourishing my body for the coming day.

October 13

Persistence is the twin sister of excellence. One is a matter
of quality; the other, a matter of time.

—Marabel Morgan

Our hunt for improved health can become exhausting, expensive, and
frustrating. We could be tempted to surrender because of the level of energy
required to obtain quality health care. The quantity of determination and
faith we possess can provide a boost by allowing us to continue even when
we are fatigued. We can consider asking a friend or family member to drive
us instead of canceling an appointment because of fatigue.

If we visit a physician who is qualified to diagnose and treat our
condition when symptoms first manifest, we can receive professional
medical assistance, which in turn could lessen the severity of our many
complications. And should a physician we frequent or various techniques
we attempt not be of benefit, we can try shifting the direction toward
natural relief. Obtaining a tolerable degree of respite from aggravating
symptoms may entail experimenting with several herbal remedies or
prescription medications while we work to find a satisfactory combination.
Even if results are achieved at a mere crawl, seeking our well-being is worth
the effort and expense.

It is through my persistence that
I begin—and continue—my healing journey.

October 14

True silence is the rest of the mind; it is to the spirit what sleep is to the body, nourishment and refreshment.
—William Penn

The physical therapist explained my assignment: go home and practice lying in a quiet room, on a solid surface (and do nothing!) for a few minutes a day. I had not realized how difficult it had become for me to relax. I was in an exceptionally stress-induced stage of my life. Overdoing it had become my unhealthy norm, and I knew that altering my approach to rest would be valuable.

Maintaining a balance between activity and stillness can be troublesome. There may be a tendency for us to push ourselves a little too far, scheduling and attempting too much and just generally overdoing life. On the other hand, excessive rest can extend our pain, tighten our muscles, and even hamper our self-confidence. It might be necessary to schedule a time for stillness as well as being active. Both are equally beneficial.

We can designate a time every day to do nothing. On days when we are unusually frazzled and fatigued, reclining with our feet elevated above our heads can be energizing. Let's try setting a timer for ten to fifteen minutes (as this is not a time to sleep, but to relax) and merely close our eyes. We are nourishing our bodies by maintaining an interval in our daily schedules for silence. By acknowledging the needs of our bodies and minds, we invite a pause.

I will rest my mind, thereby calming my spirit.

October 15

The greatest act of faith some days is to simply get up and face another day.

—Amy Gatliff

It may seem at times that those who necessitate the most significant quantity of encouragement might rarely receive it. Reaching out can be difficult even when we desire contact with others, and the nature of our illness could cause periodic isolation. The effort required to rise each morning and ready ourselves to face the world might cause us to be overwhelmed.

We may be acquainted with a person who, through attempting to deal with the effects of daily health changes, has begun to slip into a spiral of depression. We could help those who are struggling by offering encouragement (if asked) as they heal. Since we are not qualified to help professionally, we can gently refer them to a physician or counselor for assistance. Arranging an outing for tea or coffee can be mutually beneficial, and on most days, it is within our can-do range.

To gaze beyond our illness and our present lives to consider others can be rewarding. By ceasing to deliberate on our own personal problems and helping someone else face the day, we could fashion a positive, healing state of mind.

As we rise and face another day,
we can appreciate the knowledge that we are not alone

October 16

Prudence keeps life safe, but does not often make it happy.
—Samuel Johnson

Oh, we hurt so badly, and taking to our beds and staying put seems the prudent thing to do. And in light of this debilitating pain and fatigue, wouldn't extra rest be the answer? However, studies show that movement (rising and easing into our day) is valuable for chronic pain, while tempering activities with rest is an optimal goal.

When we diminish the emphasis on our wellness struggles, we liberate vitality that we can apply to whatever creates delight. Let's think happy! By considering every justification, we can choose a fun concept within our capabilities and attempt it. However, if we are unable to obtain our goal, we can shift our options—recalling that our aim is happiness. Our objective *is* achievable. When we gravitate from a self-pity rut into cheerfulness, it just feels good, and feeling good beats feeling sick any day.

I will trade in my sick bed for a smile,
with happiness as my goal.

October 17

We can lick gravity, but sometimes the paperwork is overwhelming.

—Wernher von Braun

I was deep inside one of those days that make me feel driven instead of calm, where decisions were flying back and forth, and tension was escalating. Even though I had my priority list, I began to crave immediate action and relief from the mounting obligations. Seeing me working in such a frenzy, you may have laughed at the futility of it all. Soon I admitted to myself that I was overwhelmed and decided to vacate the house of chores and get away to a nearby favorite spot, where I could sip water, relax, and look out over the calming ripples of a nearby lake.

When we realize that stress intensifies our symptoms, you would think that would be enough—that we could be even-keeled from that moment forward. Oh, if only it were that easy! It can often feel like the more focus we exert on the fact that we are overtaxed, the further exhausted we become. By adopting a new approach to recognize our enemy of stress, we smooth the way for a change. When we notice we are overwhelmed, let's try pausing, breathing gently, and (if possible) departing for a different, calmer location. In some situations, all that is necessary is a different environment to nudge us out of a maxed-out tense mood.

I will try to watch for signs of burnout and apply changes
before stress seizes a destructive hold.

October 18

The way I see it, if you want the rainbow, you gotta put
up with the rain.

—Dolly Parton

Some of us may tolerate more than our share of life's "rain." Or perhaps
we are so intent on actively shielding ourselves from life's storms that we
miss our rainbow. A degree of difficulty is to be expected occasionally in
everyone's life.

Nevertheless, if we sense that the problems in our lives outweigh the
positives, it could be beneficial to practice various relaxation exercises, such
as yoga or deep breathing. We can also try meditation, which can lower our
tension and even reduce blood pressure in individuals who are predisposed
to hypertension. Let's not make it complicated. We can merely sit still in
a chair with our eyes closed at least once a day.

Let's aim to focus on life's delights, not the hurdles, all the while
ushering in acceptance of what is. A favorable balance that leads to healing
is learning tolerance through coping skills. One key to bearing our troubles
is learning to cope. Gentle exercise and deep breathing are only a couple of
coping mechanisms we can use. We can determine a managing tool that
is most suited for us while recognizing whatever creates the multicolored
arc of happiness we call a rainbow.

I will behold my happiness rainbow today.

October 19

Guard well within yourself that treasure, kindness. Know how to give without hesitation, how to lose without regret, how to acquire without meanness.

—George Sand

We might feel now and again that no one understands us or our struggle with health issues, leading to the potential for self-pity. This type of reasoning has the potential to morph into a "woe is me" mind-set. When we look beyond our own world that involves pain, fatigue, and fibro fog, we can turn our focus elsewhere and try to spread a little kindness.

While we are waiting in a food store line, we can smile briefly at someone. We may receive a return grin or maybe not. We can try to move our attention to another person as we apply that easy yet powerful act of kindness—a smile. Oh, there it is, the unique exchange of pleasantness, brief yet potent!

There are many situations in daily exchanges with friends or even strangers where we could give of ourselves through seemingly insignificant means. To offer consideration by listening attentively during a conversation and inquiring about another can make us feel better. These connections with people can be worthwhile, and by shifting attention away from ourselves, we relinquish the hold on our concerns, welcoming additional people into our day.

I will be open to opportunities to reach out positively
to those who cross my path today.

October 20

The woods are lovely, dark and deep
But I have promises to keep
And miles to go before I sleep
And miles to go before I sleep.

—Robert Frost

Multiple studies reveal that being a night owl causes people to experience increased pain and has the potential for elevated glucose and blood pressure levels. Additionally, night owls tend to put weight on around the waist due to their late eating habits. Nonrestorative sleep and sleep disruptions are symptoms of fibromyalgia, and waking up stiff and in pain may occur the next day.

By listening to our cyclical sleep rhythm (or adjusting it) and sleeping approximately eight hours a night, we have an advantage toward achieving wellness. It is possible to shift from being a night owl to a morning person—with perseverance. We can choose the hour to wake every morning and stick to it. In a week or two, we will begin to wake up without an alarm. Next we can choose a bedtime without wavering. When we get the recommended amount of nightly sleep, our bodies will have an opportunity for repair and rejuvenation through the night. Eventually we must give ourselves permission to sleep—and the rest we sorely need will come.

I will get adequate rest,
putting aside food, work, or exercise three hours before bed.

October 21

What one does is what counts. Not what one had the intention of doing.

—Pablo Picasso

Our best intentions could backfire in unexpected ways. It may not be adequate to have planned everything out to the last detail, yet when push comes to shove, we veered in another direction. Perhaps we feel we have no choice and that people or things have interceded, forcing our decision. We always have options. When things go awry, we can devise a backup plan or simply wing it. The most useless thing for us to do is fret.

As we encounter something that affects us negatively, the way we handle it is what remains when the dust settles. Some may forget how a situation unfolded. However our action or reaction—whether composed and well thought out or brisk and spontaneous—reminds us of the power of choice and the responsibility that surrounds our decisions. We must live with our decisions, and in our best interest, a little thinking before doing can be a wise move.

My actions will be without reproach.

October 22

Like the wind crying endlessly through the universe,
Time carries away the names and the deeds of conquerors
and commoners alike.
And all that we are, all that remains, is in the memories
of those who cared we came this way for a brief moment.
—Harlan Ellison

Recalling fond memories from childhood can be a wholesome approach to our varied pasts. There are usually events that shine through as happy, fun, or at the very least, entertaining. Some of what life doles out generates delightful images and recollections. We can consciously take pleasure in these moments while enjoying that sliver of light and love in our lives.

Our remembrances are not always distinct because of sudden confusion (fibro fog) sweeping in and clouding the issues. If this is the circumstance, we could rely on a family member who can help us rediscover pleasant experiences we don't readily recall.

By carving out fresh memories full of joy and love to share with others, we provide happenings to savor in our future. Those we touch along the way form their own little gems of memory to retain. We can sprinkle kindness and generosity plentifully in our wake, for the past is but a moment in time, the future is written with invisible ink, and we can only alter the present.

I will leave a shimmering trail of love and happiness today.

October 23

It doesn't matter how much milk you spill as long as you
don't lose the cow.

—Harvey Mackay

Everyone makes blunders. Those of us with fibromyalgia may face a few
more than average because of fibro fog. When errors are unavoidable, we
can ask ourselves, "What is essential?" We can list our daily schedule into
three columns: vital, conceivable, and irrelevant. This breakdown allows
us to zero in on what is most significant, keeping us from being distracted
by life's little hiccups along the way.

We might be placing undue attention on the challenges in our lives,
thereby creating additional hassles. By directing the focus to what we
consider our priorities—whether it is wellness and fitness or a balanced
checkbook—we give essential direction to our existence. For optimum
personal growth, keeping things in perspective is a worthy goal.

I will find my focus and concentrate
on my accomplishments—not my slipups.

October 24

Live a balanced life—learn some and think some and draw and paint and sing and dance and play and work every day some.

—Robert Fulghum

When we are caught in the throes of anxious or stressful thinking or actions, it may be arduous to pull back from a dilemma. It might take a flare up before we comprehend that we are exerting ourselves to excess— but at what cost to our health? Let's try to set apart a reasonable portion of our day for work and play, easing our burdens and freeing up our ability to unwind. Because of the waxing and waning of our energy, we could habitually overdo activities that can leave little time for fun or relaxation that are so essential for the rejuvenation of body, mind, and spirit.

It takes minutiae of scheduling and the ability to step up and mold our own lives to achieve balance. Sometimes we might say no and other times it may be a yes. All the while we can retain a peaceful spirit, that crucial ingredient that is essential for offsetting imbalance, which aids in attaining a minimum of stress and a maximum of enjoyment. A worthwhile endeavor to aim for a satisfying proportion of learning, play, and work in our every day is the target.

I understand the importance of pacing myself
while continuing to enjoy life abundantly.

October 25

The greater danger for most of us is not that our aim is too
high and we miss it, but that it is too low and we reach it.
—Michelangelo

If anyone other than a physician or physical therapist advises us to abstain
from an activity, we might think, *Why or why not?* Goals keep hope
flourishing, although by not setting our objective high enough, we might
impede our sense of accomplishment. Falling short of an aim happens to
everyone at times, and by treating ourselves gently in setbacks as well as
successes, we enhance our self-confidence. With measured advancement,
we can become more active, and our scope of possibilities continues to
broaden.

Perhaps we could begin with a compilation of goals that we concede
are obtainable and then move on to our dreams and hopes. It doesn't
hurt to make a note of everything. For example, we might know that
snowboarding or skydiving may never happen for us, although by citing
them as an aspiration, we acknowledge our visions. By maintaining
an update of any goals, we ensure new endeavors for which to strive.
Nonetheless, we keep dreaming and hoping and doing.

When I create a goals list devoid of limitations,
I ensure unencumbered accomplishments.

October 26

Oh, the powers of nature! She knows what we need, and
the doctors know nothing.

—Benvenuto Cellini

There could be physicians who aspire to hang a different name on our
syndrome, dismissing the word *fibromyalgia* altogether. Finding one who
not only believes in fibromyalgia but is also not afraid to tackle it can be
a genuine challenge. A generalized pain diagnosis has the potential to
minimize our many symptoms and lead to substandard care.

We become proactive when we transfer most of the responsibility for
our health care onto ourselves. How fortunate it is if we find a physician
who remembers us from one visit to the next and is interested in our well-
being. As we acquire an enhanced perception of our condition, we begin
to recognize the limits of modern medicine and map out a personal course
for wellness, which might also include alternative care.

Along with a qualified physician, nature is a potent healing source,
soothing our wired nervous systems. Let's consider finding a tranquil place
from the hustle and bustle and gadgets and responsibilities of everyday
life, a respite where we engage in a fundamentally peaceful level through
profound influences of the natural world. One hour in nature is to how
many hours of conventional medicine? We experience healing on another
level when we emphasize embracing greenspaces.

I will be open to help from conventional medical sources
but head to nature to "forest bathe."

October 27

A keen sense of humor helps us to overlook the unbecoming, understand the unconventional, tolerate the unpleasant, overcome the unexpected, and outlast the unbearable.

—Billy Graham

I was going through a rough patch. It seemed that all that could go wrong did go wrong. My symptoms were ramping up, and I was yearning for a diversion—something lighthearted to see me through this challenging period. Having already gathered selections of funnies from newspapers and sensing the present to be the perfect time to polish up my sense of humor, I started going through my comic collection, and by the third one, I had forgotten my woes and was rocking with laughter.

Oh, those flare ups, which might include headaches and irritable bowel syndrome, can get the better of us if we let them. Choosing to laugh despite our adversities can shift the power and control of our lives—fraught with chronic medical problems—back to us. We will not feel the weight of limitations when we refuse to let life's hardships get us down. Belly laughs, those big laughs that shake our whole bodies, function as an internal massage as well as replacing any frowns with smiles. We can acknowledge the healing properties of laughter and indulge ourselves often. Even smiles create those natural painkillers (endorphins) and are a testament to a good sense of humor.

Today I will come across something to laugh about
and observe my escalating mood.

October 28

I am not afraid of storms, for I am learning how to sail
my ship.

—Louisa May Alcott

Being dependent upon others for many of our requirements might hamper
our innate sense of well-being, making an independent lifestyle more
challenging to obtain. It could become a habit, this going to others. We
stop believing in our own abilities if we are leaning on people for multiple
reasons, resulting in doubts and fears that can prevent that much-desired
succor—relaxation.

Celebrating our accomplishments, large and small, can help to shrink
many of our fears. And as we resume responsibility for our lives, we
begin our journeys back to wellness accomplishing more complex tasks
unassisted. However, having someone to depend on now and again, when
necessary, can be beneficial while we sustain our independence.

As we formulate an inventory of triumphs as well as hopes for the
future, we might encounter undiscovered goals in the process. Then,
poised to unfurl our sails of self-sufficiency, we can attempt the innovative,
while our hope in vanquishing any fears lies within our self-confidence
and independence.

My faith in my abilities will diminish any fears
and most significantly, my fear of my fibromyalgia diagnosis.

October 29

One of the most valuable things we can do to heal one another is listen to each other's stories.
—Rebecca Falls

There it goes again, that incessant ringing of the telephone. *Oh, what now?* we may think annoyingly, on a day when fatigue is at the forefront and communication is challenging. We speak a weary greeting. Our face then lights up at the recognition of the caller's voice. A friend is reaching out for human contact, and we respond in kind.

To have a friend who will also listen when we share is indeed a gift. If we have initiated a call, we can inquire whether now is convenient for a chat. If we need to foster healthy boundaries, we may indicate that we only have a few minutes to talk. By listening briefly, we can discern if a caller has an immediate need, or we may consider returning the call later.

Additionally (especially on our more problematic days), we could consider turning the telephone ringer off during meals and while sleeping, which will give us a break for much-needed repose. "Unplugging" ensures we will have an interval in which to relax and regroup and where coping with life's little ups and downs appears feasible.

I will strive to be a healing listener for someone today.

October 30

Prayer puts God's work in His hands and keeps it there.
—E.M. Bounds

The alternatives for tolerating pain and other debilitating symptoms of our illness are accessible. We could latch onto pain, make it our miserable companion, *or* we can attempt to release our hold on unpleasant symptoms and place ourselves with all our many grumbles and "why me" cries, into God's capable hands.

It may be scary initially learning to trust him, although releasing a firm grasp on discomfort and handing it over can be calming and uplifting. We might have been in the routine of dealing with our hardships unassisted, and it could be challenging to accept the possibility of unburdening ourselves and letting go of issues that are sometimes too much for us. One therapeutic exercise to lift any burdens and symptoms from our shoulders is writing letters to God, giving it all to him.

Prayer (conversation with God) is an effective pain-management strategy. It can be an asset to accept our lives with its ups and downs, if we don't take it personally when our prayers receive an answer that is not to our liking. Prayer is a powerful tool that can grant us a sense of peace (like a comforting sigh).

I will release my hold on pain through prayer.

October 31

Now and then it's good to pause in our pursuit of happiness
and just be happy.

—Guillaume Apollinaire

In a society that thinks there is a fix for everything, many often toil too
intensely at merely being happy. Some of us may make our everyday
occurrences into work—a drudgery. We may make elaborate plans, time
activities to the minute, and generally run ourselves into the ground
attempting something that could be effortless, flowing like a good novel
that we cannot put down. There are rhythms and tempos to the natural
occurrence of happiness. If we are finding cheerfulness to be just out of
reach, here are a few things we can consider:

- Do we feel undue pressure?
- Are we comparing our lives to others?
- How are we handling stress in our lives?

By fashioning a list of what makes us happy—including people, places,
and things—we can develop a more balanced, healthy approach to life.
If we are in a perpetually serious frame of mind, striving to improve
our condition, we are possibly closing the door on the fun. Let's choose
something from our happiness list and just do it! No big plans or fancy
clothes are required—only the willingness to surrender some control and
give in to joy.

I will be happy—this very moment!

November 1

The best is that which is most spontaneous or seemingly so.
—Isamu Noguchi

It happened again; my days were melding into each other because of repetition. I had reached that dreaded state of familiarity—boredom. I was turning around immediately!

Boredom can reach up and snatch us out of life into a dimension where everything becomes scripted and our days are short on diversity or spontaneity, where a gloom of sorts may settle about us without our knowledge as we fall into an ordinary life that is so mundane it may lose meaning.

Let us remain constantly curious and fearlessly adventurous. We can do the unexpected. Try leaving a day unplanned and go somewhere—anywhere—and do something diverse to shake up our world that has become tight and small from illness and carefulness. We can think new thoughts, explore new philosophies, read new books, and try new foods. What awaits, we know not, but the willingness to venture forth and discover makes the trip worthwhile.

I will watch lest I sink into that situation;
let's not even utter the word.

November 2

A hug is like a boomerang—you get it right back.
—Bil Keane

There may be occasions when we feel a bit blue, wondering when things will pick up. Perhaps a certain disconnect from others may arise, leading to the unwanted circumstance of seclusion. What might be done to transport ourselves through this quagmire, we may speculate?

There could be situations when we are in top-notch form, having an awesome day, and want to pass some of these delightful vibes on to another. Hug someone. It is one of the most gratifying therapeutic tools for well-being. There are studies on the benefits of hugging and being hugged that show the capacity of that powerful healer—physical touch. Affection, especially when shown by hugging, is a socially acceptable way to stay connected to people.

Let's try for a minimum of one hug a day (twelve is the general recommendation!), and like that apple a day, the extra benefit could be contracting fewer colds or viruses. Know an elderly neighbor? On our next encounter, let's offer a gentle hug and perchance receive the reward of a beaming smile (and a surprisingly good grip in return). This interaction by touch is known to release oxytocin (the feel-good hormone) while lowering stress hormones such as cortisol, improving moods, and brightening days.

Hugging is such a mutual affection!
I will hug someone today.

November 3

Sometimes I say the medication is even tougher than the illness.

—Sanya Richards-Ross

Pain is the primary symptom of fibromyalgia. Achieving relief with natural remedies as an alternative to chemicals sounds healthier, but even natural and herbal treatments have side effects. Any untreated pain can stir up excessive levels of stress, creating a near-constant state of distress.

If we do not manage the tension that clings to chronic illness, we can exponentially push discomfort from mild into excruciating agony. Our physicians may prescribe medication, proffered as one of the coping options available to us, while reluctance to use pharmaceuticals is understandable. On the other hand, unaddressed symptoms can heap on irritability and impatience, which can possibly become an incentive to follow through with our prescribed dosage, and when we are under a physician's care, we can gain better quality of life. Let's revisit our symptom management and consider taking a break from drugs or herbal therapy periodically, giving the liver and kidneys a much-needed break.

That's not to say that medication and herbal remedies are the only way to address our pain, fatigue, and other aggravating symptoms. Modalities such as massage, acupuncture, acupressure, and cupping have been shown to make a sizable difference in pain levels in the treatment of fibromyalgia, and we might consider these safer, drug-free approaches to symptom control.

I can manage my symptoms with dignity.

November 4

For it is in giving that we receive.
—St. Francis of Assisi

How compliments are given and received speaks volumes. Denying someone's praise is like refusing their gift. And being sparse in praising another may appear self-centered.

If we put too much emphasis on our medical problems, we might not notice a compliment when sincerely given. The ability to step out of our condition and be accepting of any gift is healthy behavior. We can try not to brush aside the kind thoughts, words, and actions of others, for these can perk up our day.

When we are on the giving end of an accolade, it feels genuinely satisfying. While giving the gift of approval to someone, we can ease the burden of ill health by inviting wellness through healthy emotions and actions. Let's glance around today, acknowledging who are the blessings in our lives and convey this message to them with gratitude.

I will enjoy the compliment, the giving, and the receiving.

November 5

With the power of soul
Anything is possible.
With the power of you
Anything you wanna do.

—Jimi Hendrix

No one ever told me I could do or be whatever I wanted. I was pointed in a very narrow direction and left to figure things out for myself. Later I found my favorite work was volunteering, especially teaching creative writing and art to grade schoolers. This seemed the most enjoyable and satisfying.

We might lack a support system, which is so helpful to the success of *any* endeavor, whether in our work or any number of activities we attempt. If a family member is unavailable for support, we can look to friends and healthcare workers or even a certified therapist. We can consider anyone who has got our back in this often-solo journey of chronic health condition to be a support connection. Often we are the ones who encourage and motivate ourselves.

Although, if need be, we can discover how to be our own support person, putting anything we want to do in the forefront. Not having to consider others' opinions or have them weigh in on our choices can be freeing, helping to establish an expanded sense of self-confidence and self-love.

Everything I touch helps shape me.
Embracing this helps me love who I am.

November 6

Look twice before you leap.

—Charlotte Bronte

Many and varied challenges lie in wait for those of us with a diminished health capacity. Everything from our daily physical activities and exercise, to formulating decisions when we are in a fog of confusion is attainable when we accept our altered way of living. We can no longer run unchecked into the wind. Doing and being has become more of a challenge as situations that necessitate a bit of caution will always exist.

Observing how and where our energies are spent—giving thoughtful pause before considering jobs such as serving on a committee or chairing a meeting—can assist in time management. Through researching what a duty entails and discerning whether a position is within the realm of our possibilities, we formulate whether it is attainable. Likewise, for errands, social events, and group outings, consideration of our capacity and physical capabilities to undertake them will prevent us from overtaxing ourselves. With a few adjustments, our many challenges might not thwart our pursuit of worthwhile exercise, hobbies, or occupations.

I will take that leap,
having due consideration of its outcome regarding my well-being.

November 7

In every conceivable manner, the family is link to our past, bridge to our future.

—Alex Haley

What are our first memories, and how do they shape us? For us to reminiscence about a happy first memory is superlative, but if our first memory is less than happy, we can skip ahead to a cheerful recollection and dub that remembrance our first. It is seldom useful to fixate on old encumbered feelings.

All our recollections are linked together like a train set and can be separated, inspected, admired, and put away when done. We continually form new memories to record and visit at will in the future, casting aside the troublesome and valuing the precious.

Our stories are personal, and maintaining our heritage in the telling keeps our lineage intact while recognizing and appreciating our family's origin. By journaling positive recollections while they are currently fresh, we keep them alive to read (silent or aloud) when we crave an uplifting story.

I will acknowledge my history that is etched like cut crystal.
With some memories appearing as cracks while others are like fine art.

November 8

When the heart has acquired stillness, it will look upon the
heights and depths of knowledge, and the intellect, once
quieted, will be given to hear wonderful things of God.

—Hesychios

Some years ago, I participated in an Introduction to Meditation class. I was
already a Christian and a spiritual person, and the thought of acquiring
increased inner peace appealed to me. I continued with it for a while and
then gradually ceased this practice. Later, I began to meditate again and
currently practice it daily. I have noticed a lowered anxiety level with a
general boost in my overall mood.

Meditation is not *thinking* but the opposite of thought and knowledge;
it is the quieting of the intellect and opening to spirituality. This action
seems counterproductive, but it is like a healing balm on a wound. There
are many helpful guides available on the subject if we are interested,
although we could pick up the art of meditation on our own.

The acquisition of a gentle heart can offer us succor in troubling
times, carrying us through many a rough patch. Having a solid spiritual
foundation is a natural buffer to stumbling blocks evoking change, some
understated yet some profound. Taking a few minutes daily to sit calmly
and be mindful is a healing gesture intent on increasing our well-being,
soothing our anxiety, and bringing about spiritual awareness.

I will meditate,
allowing peace to settle where there once was discord.

November 9

Joy is the simplest form of gratitude.

—Karl Barth

We can ask ourselves if we are displaying enough gratitude in our lives. With the burden of a chronic health diagnosis, sometimes moodiness and frowns coexist, and we don't detect our recurring state of discontent. Do we express appreciation for our family and friends? What is our method of showing gratitude?

When we take note of the face and voice we offer the world, it can provide an insight into how much joy is present in our lives. Often actions, not words, convey gratitude to others. A smile is a beautiful gift to bestow on others. It can make their day extra pleasant while adding sparkle to our own. There is no vocabulary necessary with this method of communication; smiles become gifts to circulate. A bit of cheer added to our day can speak joyful volumes of appreciation for our friends and family.

I will practice joy as a form of gratitude today.

November 10

Always do your best, your best is going to change from moment to moment; it will be different when you are healthy as opposed to sick. Under any circumstance, simply do your best and you will avoid self-judgment, self-abuse and regret.

—Miguel Angel Ruiz

Our best when we were healthier may not resemble our best today. No matter. Our circumstance has changed and our abilities along with it. Any chastising concerning our decisions is defeatist behavior.

However, if we regret any words or actions toward others, we can attempt to make amends. By expressing these feelings, there can be an ease in tension along with anxiety that may have built up around old issues. If we have done our best in a situation, analyzing our part in it (what we could have done differently) serves no useful purpose, and regrets can then take a back seat to accomplishments.

We all make mistakes, and remembering to be kind to ourselves can foster self-love. Just plugging along as best we can is the finest we can hope for as we embrace a renewed sense of freedom and a more satisfying life.

I will abandon any regrets,
knowing I did the best I could.

November 11

Life does not have to be perfect to be wonderful.

—Annette Funicello

Life in general delivers many challenges. Chronic illness patients do well when we maintain balance in our lives and accept our condition with all its complexities. We might believe that denial of our health burdens and desiring flawlessness is the only path to happiness; however; denial can exacerbate stress and affect us adversely.

Facing our lives with their blessings and tribulations helps in accepting our reality. We can begin adapting to the many changes in our limitations instead of resisting them. This can guide us along a smoother, healthier path.

By acknowledging our strengths, we can appreciate the lovely individual God created, and our lives begin to resonate with confident significance. Easing up on desiring perfection and accepting things as they are allows the wonderful to unfold.

I will strive for a wonderful life today,
not a perfect one.

November 12

The ... patient should be made to understand that he or she must take charge of his own life. Don't take your body to the doctor as if he were a repair shop.

—Quentin Regestein

How many of us have lamented, "I wish somebody could just fix me"? In the early stages of our condition, we may be caught voicing this desire. However, as time advances, we realize this is not going away. With an awareness of how powerfully our attitudes and moods shape our health, we may comprehend that the *fixing* is ours to do.

At times acting as if we are healthy and not beset with a chronic illness seems the best course. When we continue to follow our physician's advice, such as healthy sleep habits, wholesome nutrition, and gentle exercise— without dwelling upon our disadvantages—our moods can elevate. The saying, "We are only as healthy as we conceive ourselves to be" is useful. With that in mind, it bodes well to do our part in the healing process. With courage, it is possible for us to move into the uncharted territory of improvement while we are living with fibromyalgia, the elusive illness without a decided cause or cure. Are we ready?

If I merely perceive myself capable of progress,
there is a good chance that I am.

November 13

I look forward to being older, when what you look like becomes less and less an issue and what you are is the point.

—Susan Sarandon

Society appears to reward those who are blessed with youth and beauty, causing some to feel that how we look is essential and that one is judged superficially by one's exteriors, such as wardrobe or make-up. Discerning how merely to do our best and releasing any unattainable expectations can be advantageous for healthy confidence. It might be difficult to continually look and feel our best. It may require a little more effort on certain days.

The autumn of life is said to be the best there is. We are old enough to have enjoyed many experiences and young enough to appreciate still more. By making any wrinkles our friends, we can ease their onset. Consider them badges of wisdom. Let's maintain an interest in our appearance., all the while knowing that under our exterior lays the real individual, where character and wisdom rule.

By embracing each phase as we pass through it, ever becoming the unique person we have always dreamed, we accept ourselves in our present cycle of life, acknowledging our youth as well as whatever lies ahead. As we revel in the aging process, we remain conscious that with the passing of each day, we obtain a fuller understanding of life.

I will welcome each passing year with a smile,
not a groan.

November 14

A man too busy to take care of his health is like a mechanic
too busy to take care of his tools.

—Spanish proverb

The issue of when and how we use medications for the relief of our many
symptoms is frequently a concern. Discussion with our physicians enables
us to form more functional decisions. If prescriptions for pain or other
symptoms are in order, our inquiries can alert us to any potentially harmful
interactions with current medications or nutrition supplements, herbals,
and OTC treatments.

We may want to discuss the topic with our physicians and consider
an alternative to drugs by questioning what herbal remedies are available.
Herbals can also produce side effects similar to prescribed treatments.
Homeopathic preparations are OTC, highly diluted nontoxic substances
(usually pellets or liquids), which can be taken to trigger the body's natural
system of healing. Because of the minute dosage, there are generally few to
no ill effects, which is a boon to those who cannot tolerate conventional
medicine. We are in a stronger position to make rational assessments of
our health requirements when we research all possibilities.

I will be straightforward and honest about my medical needs,
which can open the door to healthy alternatives.

November 15

Healing is embracing what is most feared;
healing is opening what has been closed,
softening what has hardened into obstruction,
healing is learning to trust life.

— Jeanne Achterberg

In addition to a chronic medical condition, some of us may have the added obstacle of a family member with alcohol or drug problems. Support groups specific to these issues have been known to assist recovery for people who have friends or family members struggling with addictions. In most cities, there are meetings available to attend where individuals with similar stories and understanding, meet for mutual support.

If our lives are affected by the alcohol or drugs habits of others, we can choose to reach out for reassurance and understanding today. The stories sound familiar, and the smiles and hugs can bring comfort to a possibly bewildering situation as we feel the loving welcome radiating from the gathering. Attending one of these support groups can foster healing and help us regain the ability to trust life again.

I can attend a support group
if I am concerned about a family member's drug habits,
promoting a healthier pattern of living for myself.

November 16

Good timber does not grow with ease. The stronger the
wind, the stronger the trees.

—Willard Marriott

Some days we seem to be walking into a stiff wind, getting nowhere. We
may feel a multitude of emotions: anxiety, fear, confusion, or anger—to
name a few. Despite these compelling feelings, we are capable of preventing
overwhelming bouts of despair from dominating, thereby gaining in
emotional strength.

Regardless of our physical condition, we can continue to progress
emotionally and spiritually. Acknowledging our feelings is the first step in
dealing with them. By the acceptance of our chronic health condition and
the accompanying complications, our occasional flagging self-confidence
can be bolstered. We can acquire a, "Whew, I made it through a challenging
flare up, and I can make it through anything" disposition. This is character
strengthening. From here, we embark on our journeys toward wellness,
starting with the acceptance of and coping with our various symptoms.

I will accept my condition, however difficult,
for this is part of coping that will make me stronger.

November 17

I get up. I walk. I fall down. Meanwhile, I keep dancing.
—Hillel

It was autumn in the Deep South. The air was clear and crisp, and I was delighted to be out walking. After several falls earlier that year, I required the occasional assistance of a cane. I was strolling (albeit slowly) down a street lined on both sides with stunning live oaks, with Spanish moss like nature's ornaments dripping from massive limbs. The trees met over the road, making an archway of magnificence. I may have been moving slower than usual, but in doing so, I had ample opportunity to take in my picturesque surroundings.

If we are fortunate to be able to walk (unaided or with the help of an assistive device), we usually are a bit more cautious if we have previously taken a tumble. We can continue to appreciate walking outdoors, being mindful of where we step, while likewise taking in the grandeur that is God's green earth. We can grab a friend, family member, or pet and head for the great outdoors on foot, breathing in the day and enjoying a pleasurable outing. Let's do a mental jig for joy, welcoming the fresh air and our capacity to enjoy it.

My attitude speaks volumes,
and a good one can carry me along.

November 18

There is something about a closet that makes a skeleton terribly restless.

—Wilson Mizner

We all carry personal baggage from our past. That closet with the skeleton or baggage is ours for keeps. There are those who prop open the closet door, exposing everything, frequently dragging it all out. However, to be stuck in the past reduces forward motion and may delay essential healing. We could shove those skeletons into a distant place, one that we don't visit or think about every day.

By remembering our family events without emphasizing the negatives, we might be able to extract the sting from them. If we listen to friends share some of their stories, we will probably grasp that everyone has their drama. A good solution is to try to concentrate on recollections that don't trigger bad memories and insert a new ending to our more problematic stories. By keeping busy with work, hobbies, or a social life, we can avoid getting bogged down in the dread. When we realize everyone has those stories (or skeletons if you will), we may be able to handle our own with greater ease.

I will look for the humor in my own story.

November 19

We do not remember days; we remember moments.
—Cesare Pavese

We can feel realistic anticipation when we are facing holidays and family celebrations or dread. If we have inflated expectations, this can impede our enjoyment of a festive event. Detailed and occasionally elaborate preparation weeks or months in advance may expend our energy. At the close of the holiday season, baffling disappointment and possibly depression may take root if we do not pace ourselves a bit.

If we are feeling overwhelmed when we attend holiday events, we could try excusing ourselves from the center of activity and locating a quiet corner (try earplugs) for a time of repose and renewal. We can close our eyes if only briefly, allowing a pause for rebooting. Afterward we can rejoin the festivities refreshed. During a celebration, we can join in brief, lighthearted conversations, taking an interest in others. By limiting our contribution to a reasonable length, we can engage in the festivities, participating in games or group activities as able. By the gathering of specific holiday moments, we form happy remembrances to treasure.

I will create some moments to cherish.

November 20

I get up and bless the light thin clouds and the first
twittering of birds, and the breathing air and smiling
face of the hills.

—Giacomo Leopardi

Are we greeting each day with thanksgiving and admiration? Perhaps we
are prone to be in a slight fog and fatigued, with tight muscles or pain in
the morning. We may be slow to smile at those we share space with and
more reluctant still to appreciate our day.

Leaving a small prayer or encouraging note at our bedside that we
can read upon rising can help provide a supportive spiritual experience.
Adopting a change in our manner, such as awakening and blessing the
day, can be an expression of gratitude. Even our pets will welcome our
improved morning attitude.

Let's open wide our shades or curtains first thing (whatever the
weather) and greet the day. We can pause, listening for the trill of a bird
or perhaps the cadence of a rain shower. And as we begin our day with an
upbeat attitude, we encourage a positive atmosphere to permeate our being.

I will arise, breathe in, and ... smile!

November 21

I made a mistake today,
I made a mistake yesterday.
I think it's ... very important to ignore the negative.
—Jerry Rubin

Like all our muscles, the brain must be exercised to perform at its peak. By continuing to read, learn, and have stimulating conversations, we facilitate less confusion in our daily interactions. Merely conversing with others about current events or any topic of interest can be a worthy challenge when we are experiencing occasional cognitive difficulties.

Confusion and mistakes are sporadic occurrences for everyone; although we face more than the average person, we need not explain or defend ourselves. We made a mistake. Move on. The world does not revolve around every word we speak. We may discover people usually forgive conversational errors, and we are frequently our worst critic. If we learn to relax when communicating with others, we start to be ourselves. This includes confused moments in addition to our numerous moments of clarity.

I will focus on the upbeat, not the downbeat.

November 22

Skills vary with the man. We must ... strive by that which
is born in us.

—Pindar

We may perceive the talents of others yet discover it is difficult to recognize
our own gifts. We all have abilities and talents that are only awaiting
recognition. Compiling a list of our interests and accomplishments and
then acknowledging a common thread is a useful technique for identifying
our skills. Or we could ask a good friend what talents we innately possess.

Do we have an ear for music? It is not necessary to be a concert pianist
to possess musical abilities. Perhaps we have a flair for cooking. This
pleasurable (and valuable for independent living) pursuit can generate
tasty results. We possibly work effortlessly with the elderly or children.
Volunteering our time to assist in these areas can bring about gratification.

Uncovering a forgotten aptitude that has lain dormant is an opportunity
in the making. We merely need to tap into this ability to acquire the
rewards. We may be amazed to realize that many of our dreams are within
our reach when we employ talents we already possess.

I am an accomplished person;
I will utilize an aptitude today.

November 23

Not what we say about our blessings, but how we use
them, is the true measure of our thanksgiving.
—W.T. Purkiser

On Thanksgiving Day, going around the table and expressing what we
are grateful for in our lives is a shared tradition in many a home. This
sharing can lead to a curious mixture of tears, whether of joy or sadness
and often mutual joking. The gathering is usually our family and friends;
they know our trials and discern our blessings. They recognize the ones
who may proffer a path or a situation but are lacking in gratitude for their
many advantages.

Are we telling one story and living another? If we claim happiness,
smiles and laughter frequently erupt with ease. If we extol on the pleasure
of our work, we will emit a radiant delight. Advantages we may have
previously overlooked can be realized by discovering and identifying our
little miracles—an exercise in genuineness. We can again give thanks while
adding new findings to the blessings that have already been bestowed
on us.

I will give thanks for my many blessings
and not squander a single precious one.

November 24

Courage is the ladder on which all other virtues mount.
—Clare Boothe Luce

Anyone with a chronic medical problem is a walking statement of the courage and fearlessness that is basic to face every day. This is an asset. We need only to discover how to use this virtue. From diagnosis onward, we face an uphill battle with a misunderstood illness. But do we feel courageous? Maybe we do not. But we are.

To identify our moments of courage, let's begin by composing a list of our problematical times encountered and solved during the past week. Alongside each challenging occurrence, recount how the issue was resolved. This resolution list will reveal that even the smallest inconveniences often require mettle to overcome them.

When we rely on courage, we can fashion more adaptable lives, bringing us a greater sense of well-being and self-worth. We can welcome the positive changes that will occur when we apply courage to our lives.

I will acknowledge my moments of courage.

November 25

Now if I had an Indian name, it would be "Stands in Confusion."

—Caroline Lawrence

Are we befuddled by periodic confusion, otherwise known as fibro fog? These temporary mix-ups may express themselves in different behaviors, such as losing or misplacing items. First, we have our glasses; then, poof, they're gone!

Misplacing our eyeglasses can be an unpleasant incident because the world becomes fuzzy and everyone may be out of focus. But if we can maintain a sense of humor about our confusion, we learn a graceful method of coping with this frequently upsetting symptom of our medical condition.

Let's go easy on ourselves when we are dealing with fibro fog, for we appreciate that the forgetfulness and jumbled words will soon be replaced with increased clarity. Confusion can worsen with tension and anxiety. Acquiring the skill of relaxation in the throes of fibro fog can thwart its potency, making way for humor in our day.

I will lighten up should fibro fog visit today,
keeping my sense of humor intact.

November 26

I still miss those I loved who are no longer with me but I find I am grateful for having loved them. The gratitude has finally conquered the loss.

—Rita Mae Brown

Friends and acquaintances may come and go in our lives. Perhaps our children or relatives live far from our home. The divorce rate is high, and couples do not always try to resolve their differences. Everything and everyone around us seems to be in flux. No one escapes the grief that loss creates. The list of casualties may start with our health, job, or spouse in addition to many of our capabilities.

Being grateful for having known and loved those we have lost through distance or death eases the heartache we endure, emphasizing the haves, not the have-nots. It is through a healthy attitude and maintaining emotional balance despite losses that we avert depression from engulfing us. By continuing to form relationships, we expose ourselves to a measure of healthy risk-taking.

I will contemplate my gratitude, not my losses.

November 27

You can't always get what you want
But if you try sometimes
You just might find
You get what you need.

—Mick Jagger and Keith Richards

Ever feel as if happiness is unobtainable? We might review our standards and attempt to ease into acceptance of what *is*. An efficient way to begin is by accepting ourselves as we are at this very moment, right here, right now. By acknowledging our specific accomplishments, of which we all possess some, we can self-validate.

Have we attended a school or earned a GED, raised children, created art, worked inside/outside the home, or been a homemaker? Could our dreams have become altered because of challenging health issues?

Should an inventory be comprised of wants and another of *needs*, possibly there will be two comparatively similar listings. When we create superior personal moments, we garner more satisfaction rather than looking to others to fill our needs or dreams.

I value fulfilling my wants and needs daily.

November 28

God's gifts put man's best dreams to shame.
—Elizabeth Barrett Browning

I was out for a quick drive to the market, and as I rounded a corner ... Wow! I was looking directly into an incredible sunset. My camera was at home. I slowed, watching the spectacular canvas unfold in the heavens. Frequently when a sunset of breathtaking beauty occurs, I realize that perhaps it is intended for pure enjoyment at that moment, not to be recorded except in my mind.

When we are immersed in our illness as it were, buried under a mound of pain and fatigue, we may become shortsighted. The weight and the sheer burden spawned by fibromyalgia can limit our activities and impressions of our often-beautiful world, which in turn may produce excessive looking inward. By gazing around and taking in something of nature, we can generate a pause in our cycle of symptoms. And through sharing our vista with friends or family, we welcome added levity and joy into our today.

I can appreciate God's gifts
for the healing balm they proffer my fibromyalgia symptoms.

November 29

Life is 10 percent what you make it and 90 percent how
you take it.

—Irving Berlin

What we say and do can disclose more about us than we may realize. Stress
has a cumulative effect when we overreact or have an adverse response
to everyday occurrences, and our attitudes can make a difference in
everything we encounter.

Here are some suggestions for stress reduction. First, consider
purchasing a device (with earbuds) that will enable us to listen to calming
or uplifting music when we are delayed in a physician's office. By storing
reading material in our automobile, we can turn a traffic jam into a
composed and relaxing pause. Having our radio tuned to a calming music
station adjusted softly can be a buffer against the tensions of driving or
being a passenger. And if we are caught in a slight delay, such as a store
checkout line, we might gaze at the magazine headlines at the checkout
(some quite funny) or enjoy people-watching. By turning our thoughts to
the agreeable and letting go of the obstructions in our lives, we release our
hold on stress and encourage healthful living.

I will adopt an upbeat attitude
when dealing with life's stressors.

November 30

Journal writing is a voyage to the interior.
—Christina Baldwin

"What did you do yesterday?" When faced with this simple inquiry, we may look back at the asker and respond, "I can't remember." Cognitive symptoms can cause our memories to dip in and out, leaving us feeling like we have lost a few IQ points when in reality it is fibro fog, a recurrent but fleeting symptom that is worsened by anxiety.

Journaling is a simple activity that knows no rules and keeps no score. The recording of our daily events and thoughts is a creative tool for the chronically ill. Knowing our journals are for our eyes alone, we can pursue this useful method of unloading the tumultuous times as well as the beautiful moments in our everyday lives. It is a means of keeping track, of connecting with ourselves. Even on the confusing and fatiguing days, when our words are jumbled and misspelled, we can manage to record at the minimum a brief notation that is descriptive of our feelings and our day. When we are beset with confusion, a sentence scrawled upon a page can become something of a revelation, marking the unfolding of our lives.

I will let pen flow on paper and profit from my results.

December 1

This is the day which the Lord hath made; we will rejoice
and be glad in it.

—Psalm 118:24

Can we glance out at a day with a light rain shower (without lightning,
of course), grab rain gear, and head out into the weather? Splashing in
puddles can be fun! A gentle kicking of acorns or pebbles turns into an
amusing exercise. Very often in the presence of light precipitation, we will
have a park trail or sidewalk to ourselves, as many opt for only sunshine
in which to enjoy nature.

When we are out in drier conditions, we can scoop up a handful of
leaves and watch them gradually sail back to earth. Tiptoe up to a chipmunk
or small ground animal and observe their nervous eating mannerisms. See
if we can name the avian species that flies overhead, and if the bird calls
out in song, let's try to answer its call. The basic idea is to get outdoors and
notice the many diverse gifts in our environment.

As we are out and about in delightful observation, we might discern a
lessening of our pain and a smile supplanting a frown. To merely wander
outside our door in the fresh air can create joy in abundance—if we allow
it. Venturing out in the elements and noticing the simple to spectacular
gifts God has bestowed on the earth and rejoicing therein can bring respite
when it's most needed.

A smile is waiting for me in
every flower's blossom,
every tree's branch,
and every creature's call.

December 2

Happiness belongs to the self-sufficient.

—Aristotle

Empowerment! It's the gift of attending to the most significant part of our self-care at every opportunity. Self-pity can set in if we are not cognizant of the importance of providing for ourselves whenever possible. Granted, there are days when having a friend or family member help out can be a lifesaver. However, when we maintain a balance between procuring assistance when it is vital and a dependent lifestyle, this can provide a sense of well-being.

A few ideas for independence are having a support bar installed to use when we step into and out of a shower or bathtub, wearing comfortable walking shoes, and maintaining our driver's license or ability to get around by public transportation. Shopping for our own needs generates an additional sense of freedom and accomplishment. When we achieve anything personally, our well-being and happiness flourish, resulting in a feeling of individual triumph.

Today I will expand my happiness through my self-reliance.

December 3

I am still determined to be cheerful and happy, in whatever
situation I may be; for I have also learned from experience
that the greater part of our happiness or misery depends
upon our dispositions, and not upon our circumstances.
—Martha Washington

Some days I appear to float along on a sort of happiness cloud, and on
others, I really struggle to deal as irritability may battle for top billing in
my day.

What can we do when we are facing that occasional morning that
opens with grouchiness? Some techniques for coping with moodiness are
getting out of the house and going somewhere we enjoy while accepting
whatever weather and sights we incur.

There will always be options for shaping the hour into something more
desirable, but what about occasions when we are not feeling up to leaving
our homes? If we are experiencing a flare up or overwhelming fatigue,
we can try taking a time-out and listening to favorite music, reading a
favorite book, or perusing through treasured mementos. These helpful
pauses might be enough to propel us toward a more pleasant outlook, for
our benefit as well as the individuals we encounter. It may not be easy, but
it will be worth it.

Happiness—it's a choice.

December 4

If you obey all the rules, you miss all the fun.

—Katherine Hepburn

I have already made several adjustments to my lifestyle owing to fibromyalgia, and I recognize there might be more to come. My skin has been sensitizing (leading to irritation), a symptom of my condition, and I contemplated why the softer side of a T-shirt or sleep tee was on the outside. I found if I flipped it inside out before donning it, I could feel significant comfort on days when I was experiencing increased sensitivity.

There may be situations when it's not necessary to follow the rules. Often there are either voluntary or societal guidelines that make no sense when our ease or comfort are at stake. We might question who wrote these parameters, and do they make sense in our lives?

It is the subtle dictates we are speaking of, the ones that don't concern people as much as we think they do. We can vote for our well-being and break a few rules if we must. Most likely no one will notice. Often when given a choice between conformity and creative comfort, doing what is healthiest for our lifestyles can be the best decision.

Today I will formulate necessary changes
for my comfort and enjoyment.

December 5

Success on any major scale requires you to accept responsibility ... in the final analysis, the one quality that all successful people have ... is the ability to take on responsibility.

—Michael Korda

Responsibilities continue. They usually do not wait for health problems or even fatigue to lift. Most of us have some measure of obligation in our lives; this may vary at times, from a scale of what is timely to what we can postpone. Here are some questions to consider concerning responsibility.

- Are we hesitant to try new activities or work projects?
- Do we frequently tackle tasks because we think no one else can do them as well?
- Are we quick to point out all the reasons we cannot do a task or activity?
- Do we fill our lives with others' responsibilities?

Let's compile a list of all we consider our obligations and then read through them, asking, "Do we enjoy this task?" We may be surprised by our findings, leading us to discover if we are genuinely accountable and where to focus our efforts. As we add responsibilities, our accountability can receive the reward of the feelings of success that often accompany it.

I will accept responsibility, careful not to overdo it.

December 6

Figuring out what we need to do is not the challenge. The challenge is figuring out when to do it.

—Peter Turla

The beginning of our day can sometimes be an enormous hurdle. Morning is often a time of slow starts. Just the actions of preparing ourselves for the day are frequently exhausting. Once we begin our daily tasks, having a brief written plan to work from can help us determine what is necessary and what we can delay. This list can also serve as our memory aid.

Errands that we separate into manageable pieces can better assist those of us with chronic health issues. Deciding a time to begin a task and end it can give us attainable goals; this lessens the risk of overtaxing ourselves and developing or increasing pain from prolonged sitting. By setting the alarm, we can be freed from clock watching, allowing the opportunity for another activity. As we use coping tools, we can approach our tasks with a sense of satisfaction and organization.

With a little organization,
I can make better use of my scheduling.

December 7

Each day comes bearing its own gifts. Untie the ribbons.
                                        —Ruth Ann Schabacker

With the arrival of each new day, we can focus on what may be right in our world, as opposed to what might be wrong. Chronic illness can then become something we live with but not all that we are. As an outcome, health or sickness will no longer define or label who we are as individuals.

The natural world always has new and exciting revelations. To discover these lavish gifts, most of us can merely walk outside or gaze out a window. By opening our eyes to the splendor of each new day, a sense of well-being and joy can be ours. God's marvelous palette displaying flora and fauna is indeed a gift for enjoyment. Even an overcast day with its diffused light has its own beauty as we pause to embrace our organic surroundings.

We can purchase an inexpensive pocket camera and take it along on our walks. It might come as a surprise that while we are engaged in snapping photographs, our pain levels may decrease. This creative activity will leave us with something pleasurable and perhaps beautiful to behold when we later view our handiwork.

Through the appreciation of my surroundings,
I can value the gifts that each new day brings.

December 8

If we were logical, the future would be bleak indeed. But
we are more than logical. We are human beings, and we
have faith, and we have hope.

—Jacques Cousteau

I recently searched the archives of a prominent northeastern publication
and was dismayed that there was only one article printed about fibromyalgia
and that was from many years prior. I felt the wind go out of my sails and
thought, *What's the point?* Then I realized that with no new developments
in treatment for fibromyalgia, there is not much interest in printing
anything further. I leaned heavily onto my faith and hoped for additional
research and findings concerning our perplexing syndrome.

With medical research unable to unravel the mysteries of fibromyalgia,
we may despair that our future is bleak indeed. In the meantime, a
healthier approach would be for us to believe there *is* hope and search
with persistence for management and coping methods of our disorder.

Having spiritual faith and using prayer has shown to improve the lives
of the chronically ill. While we are in a flare up, it is often difficult to have
patience while waiting for an answer to our prayers. We may receive an
answer of, "Wait" or "Not now." By possessing hope and taking an active
part in our healing, we encourage a serene, brighter tomorrow.

My hope and faith are my foundation.

December 9

Do what you can, with what you have, where you are.
—Theodore Roosevelt

There could be a portion of us who are pursuing the ideal family, relationship, job, car, or home. If this has been our approach, we can step back and contemplate what we envision for ourselves (that is currently lacking) and then re-evaluate our wants. Is it possible to be satisfied with the present day, devoid of any anxiety about our future?

Listing our skills, accomplishments, and activities on paper can assist with recognizing the positives we now enjoy. If our recollections are sporadic, we can also inquire of a close friend or family member as to what activity seemed to provide us with the most pleasure over the years. Perhaps we can enjoy past pleasures once again or adapt to accepting the present as is with a willingness to accept change.

There might be satisfactory aspects of our lives that we previously overlooked while focusing on maintaining our health that come to light. Acknowledging we have health challenges, though not concentrating exclusively upon them, helps acceptance of the now become something not just hoped for but realized.

I will find something to appreciate in my present circumstances.

December 10

I'm really into good nutrition and keeping healthy!
That said, I'm, also addicted to candy—it's my biggest
weakness.

—Kina Grannis

With so many directories on how to manage pain, improve digestion,
maintain a sensible body mass index, and have more energy, we can
encounter a burden of conflicting nutritional information. We all are
familiar with the basics of what constitutes a nutritious meal, although
the pressure to improve ourselves can at times lead us to forgo treats, and
then a mere indulgence may get out of control.

It takes discipline to eat right consistently. We can consider consulting
a nutritionist to guide us in our efforts to eliminate or decrease problems
with digestion and get assistance with substitutes for food sensitivities or
allergies. It's not rocket science, but it might take working with a qualified
specialist to assist with what to eat and what to pass up.

There are always treats that we can add as a part of a good, nutritious
meal plan. If we take pleasure in the planning and preparing of a meal,
eating healthier may be less of a burden as many available books are
offering anti-inflammatory and special dietary needs. So, let us eat, drink,
and be merry, but in everything, let there be moderation.

My health and nutrition go hand in hand,
but a treat is part of the package.

December 11

Bravery is believing in yourself, and that is something no one can teach you.

—El Cordobes

Fibromyalgia can take a formerly confident person and seriously shake up his or her confidence. What was stable could become unsteady. On occasion we appear like a ship without a sail, seemingly at the mercy of our circumstances and symptoms. It can take a while to learn to accomplish what was previously a given. A few helpful tools to enhance our faltering self-esteem are to create our daily schedules based on our necessities; try something new and pat ourselves on the back for attempting it; create a can-do list consisting of our realities, such as I can sing, I can be a good friend or parent, I can type; or attend a function or activity that interests us on our own.

It can be empowering when we discover how to rely upon ourselves. As we begin to lean less on others, we can experience an expansion of well-being, bringing our self-esteem to full blossom.

I believe in my accomplishments.

December 12

Reading about nature is fine, but if a person walks in the woods, and listens carefully, he can learn more than what is in books, for they speak with the voice of God.
—George Washington Carver

I was thankful to be out walking in a local wooded park, featuring an abundant oasis of wildlife and trees in every season. A rustle in the dried grasses, a squirrel scurrying up a tree, and a cardinal chirping midwinter all bring smiles of peace and joy. This open space is special. It's my favorite to frequent and meander along the river. My prayers came quietly yet swiftly, spilling out into the tranquil stillness. When God's handiwork surrounds me, I often speak to him and pause to listen for his inner guidance.

Health issues may sidetrack us occasionally, and as a result, we may neglect to observe nature's many blessings. It might be challenging to acknowledge nature's bounty. We may be city dwellers or temporarily housebound, although most cities have areas of trees, shrubs, and grass and at the very least one park to frequent.

Have we been for a walk in nature lately no matter the season? Do we admire the variety of trees and foliage, each having their distinctive flair? Some are simple and unassuming, while others are flamboyant and incredibly bright. Even in winter, a treasure awaits us as most trees stand out against the gray sky, bold, leafless—beautiful. Are we taking time today to lighten our spirits by listening for the natural world's melodies and marveling in its spectacles?

I will gaze outside my illness
and become mindful of the many blessings nature has to offer.

December 13

I know that you believe you understand what you think
I said, but I'm not sure you realize that what you heard is
not what I meant.

—Robert McCloskey

Attempting to explain fibro fog is seldom helpful because of most people saying they too have this confusion. Yes, at some time or another everyone encounters mild confusion. Even in the face of fibro fog (a frequently dreaded symptom of our illness), we can relax and note that we are not alone. If we accept the existence of our mix-ups, it could create a more laid-back, tension-free environment. A relaxation with others can develop as communication leads to freedom to be us, including moments of disorientation as well as moments of clarity.

We undoubtedly have faced those funny and occasionally embarrassing circumstances when unintentional weird words can spring from our mouths while we are experiencing fibro fog. Let's attempt a lighter approach when we are confronted with these faux pas instances. Invent some tongue twisters with a friend or a child in the family and have some fun. We can continue repeating them until we make a blunder. At first we may be hesitant to make mistakes, but if we relax, silliness and laughs will soon follow.

I will try some tongue twisters today
and enjoy a welcoming laugh.

December 14

If instead of a gem, or even a flower, we should cast the
gift of a loving thought into the heart of a friend, that
would be giving as the angels give.
                              —George MacDonald

Are we aware of how powerful our thoughts can be? Whether affectionate
and giving or the opposite—loathing of others or ourselves—what we
think affects us. When we wish a person well by prayers or wholesome
thinking, we receive as well as give, for our outlooks shape our actions and
expressions. By desiring the best for ourselves and thinking positively of
others, we establish a healthy vision.

   As we send a loving thought into the heart of a friend, we ask God to
deliver a unique gift direct from our hearts to theirs. It needn't be lengthy.
Merely a brief caring, internal hug will do. By connecting with others
in an open-handed manner, we minimize worrying over any slights we
might perceive. And through addressing pleasant thoughts, we can enjoy
decreased tension and increased serenity. From time to time, we can divert
ourselves from our problems and focus on a deserving friend; this is a gift
of love.

I will send loving thoughts to someone today.

December 15

Clouds come floating into my life, no longer to carry rain
or usher storm, but to add color to my sunset sky.
                                    —Rabindranath Tagore

We all experience troubling times. For some, it may be our diminished
health and for others daily hardships. However, if we push ourselves too
intensely, a flare up of our symptoms can often be the outcome. If we
maintain a worrisome routine or activity, this action can initiate pain and
bring about an increase in our other symptoms.

Managing some of those minor difficulties before they become
insurmountable can aid in keeping occurrences in perspective. Exhaustion
can force us to halt, and we have time to be still for more than a moment
and absorb our surroundings—perhaps by taking in a sunset or sunrise.
This pause is an optimal opportunity to seize the pleasurable, recognizing
our many blessings while acknowledging the heavens and all the wonder
they hold.

I will see the good when I am at my worst.

December 16

Animals don't lie. Animals don't criticize. If animals have
moody days, they handle them better than humans do.
— Betty White

Our pets take us as we are, but on occasion, family members and friends
may not be as accepting. We might encounter one who frequently points
out when they think we are in the wrong. Learning to respond to criticism
with a gentle, "You might be right," can sometimes douse rising emotional
flames before they become damaging. Overthinking any rash comments
could bring anxiety to the forefront, a symptom best left unruffled.

We can consider if a judging comment from another could be accurate,
then contemplate whether a change in an area is required (considering the
source). Afterward, without stressing or obsessing, we can either toss it
away as an untruth or let it prod us into positive change.

Relationships could be lovelier
if criticisms are left at the door.

December 17

Our greatest glory consists not in never falling, but in rising every time we fall.

—Nelson Mandela

In my years of struggling with faltering health, I have taken many a fall, twisting and spraining both ankles on multiple occasions. One particularly injurious fall kept me in a wheelchair for a couple of weeks. Painful tender points made crutches unbearable. I considered purchasing a walker. I improved and trusted the help of physical therapy. I eased back into a walking routine to get me once more on my feet.

As we grapple with hurdles that may set us back physically, we can concentrate on recovery instead of getting mired in our hardships. We may have to seek the help of a physical therapist now and again for assistance to regain the loss of function or recover from an injury or a fall. This valuable time can be spent learning new and beneficial ways to exercise, walk, stretch, and move that are designed to assist with rapid recovery and ease of movement. Continuing routine light workouts coupled with some gentle stretching can tone and strengthen our muscles, bolstering wellness, renewing vigor, and preventing future injuries. We benefit from the positives we engage in through a proactive approach to our healing

I will focus on my recovery, not my injuries.

December 18

When dark December glooms the day,
And takes our autumn joys away ...

—Sir Walter Scott

The winter months with their reduced daylight and often-dreary weather can be challenging. We not only have cold temperatures to contend with, but the lack of sunshine can also sometimes lead, if not to depression then to a general feeling of malaise. We may consider having a physician test our vitamin D level to rule out a deficiency (which can cause lethargy and increased pain levels, among other problems).

We can help lift our moods by opening our blinds or curtains to invite in more light when it makes its brief winter appearances. While we are waiting for the sun to show its face, we can try full-spectrum light bulbs that provide naturally balanced illumination that can lend a hand in elevating our spirits. When we are gifted with a day resolute with rays of sunlight, let's welcome it, bundle up, and head outdoors, even if only for a short interval. The sun is uplifting and healthy in moderation, and it can often chase away the harshest of realities.

I will tackle the winter blues with a visit outdoors
to welcome winter's daily light.

December 19

Fail not to call to mind, in the course of the twenty-fifth of this month, that the finest heart that ever walked the earth was born on that day; and then smile and enjoy yourselves for the rest of it; for mirth is also of Heaven's making.

—Leigh Hunt

Let's not lose the meaning of Christmas when it seems the whole world is caught up in some frantic type of sprint this time of year. Or at least that is what it can feel like if we are so weighed down with shopping, baking, and social obligations that we leave little time to reflect on the merry side of Christmas.

We might try a new approach to the Christmas season by taking a step back from the craziness this year, one that can leave us joyful and indeed merry. We can put aside our burdens, making time for beloved choral ensembles, live nativity scenes, and special worship services. After attending seasonal celebrations, we may have an uplifted mood as we engage in smiles and share laughter with our families and friends. It doesn't matter if the cookies are store bought and the gifts are simple yet thoughtful. When our emotions have risen from despair, our hearts are free to express happiness.

I will laugh and make merry,
for it is a gift to behold in one another.

December 20

From time to time, to remind ourselves to relax, to be
peaceful, we may wish to set aside some time for a retreat,
a day of mindfulness, when we walk slowly, smile, drink
tea with a friend, and enjoy being together as if we are the
happiest people on Earth.

—Thich Nhat Hanh

For normals, an occasional day of relaxation may suffice. However, those
of us with fibromyalgia may find that we need to spend some time relaxing
every day. Learning to unwind can prevent us from being overwhelmed
and give us protection from a flare up. It's tough to be in pain, and learning
to lighten our moods can be beneficial.

Relaxation is a skill that, when acquired, can easily be repeated daily
for optimum benefits. We could begin by designating a daily time in
which to clear our schedules and our commonly encumbered minds. As
we delight in the feeling of not fixating on problems and experience being
in the moment, we might feel a smile edging forth.

Let's not engage in guilt that we should be busy but release the need
for things to be different and accept how they are right now. Time devoted
to mindfulness through daily leisure, whether alone or with a companion,
is time well spent.

Today I will remind myself to relax;
it can begin with something as simple as a smile.

December 21

Life is not what it's supposed to be. It's what it is. The way
you cope with it is what makes the difference.

—Virginia Satir

For those of us who are trying to carry on while facing chronic medical
issues, a social invitation occasionally results in a reluctant, automatic
decline. When it is necessary to graciously opt out, it may be what is best for
us. However, repeated begging off could lead to a cessation of invitations.
Instead of a firm no, we might consider the alternative, responding that
we can try to attend for a half hour or hour. This pronouncement leaves
us wiggle room as well as the pleasure of enjoying a social engagement
without becoming overtaxed.

There are ways we can take care of ourselves while additionally
interacting with others by adapting doable coping methods. One area
that is in our control is the way we dress and the footwear we choose. By
rendering these comfortable, we can ease our pain and discomfort.

We may discover creative new methods to continue a social life.
Perhaps cutting back on some activities but not all is a practical approach.
Viable events may replace previous, no longer possible, ones. And while
we recognize the necessity to pace ourselves, maintaining our vitality, we
profit when we succeed in accepting invitations.

It is what it is,
and I will cope with it today.

December 22

Don't envy me; I have my own pains.

—Barbra Streisand

Who are we to know another's story? Could we be viewing a face they only present to the outside world? We have no actual knowledge about others except what they choose to reveal. That we have fibromyalgia is not easy for others to recognize when they meet us because we look *fine*. Great even! Some of us are pretty good at hiding our pain levels from others.

Everyone has their challenges. We can routinely shift our attention to some of the positives in our lives, such as good friends, a thoughtful family member, or a sweet pet to cuddle.

A useful tool to keep envy at bay is taking periodic inventories of our accomplishments and achievements. Concentrating on our abilities with an optimistic approach leaves scant time to compare ourselves to anyone. When we bring our successes to mind if we hit a snag, we can enlist a friend or family member who gets us to help shine a light on our triumphs.

Today I will keep the spotlight on the positives in my life.

December 23

Experience is not what happens to you; it is what you do
with what happens to you.

—Aldous Huxley

We cannot undo what might, unfortunately, be an adverse piece of our
history. It is possible, however, to alter our present living conditions if they
are not health inducing. If necessary, we can modify whom we spend time
with, prompting a healthier lifestyle and amplified self-esteem.

Everyone deserves to be treated with dignity, respect, and kindness—
in words and actions. Leaving upsetting memories in the past releases
their harmful hold on us. We can then take control of our lives and adopt
a healing attitude that is soothing and self-nurturing and contributes
positively to our self-esteem and well-being. Stepping into the future with
a clearer understanding of what we require for our greater good is a start
to learning from our experiences.

I will choose a healthy "good for me" path
and not repeat a painful past.

December 24

Aerodynamically, the bumblebee shouldn't be able to fly, but the bumblebee doesn't know it, so it goes on flying anyway.

—Mary Kay Ash

People with good intentions occasionally insist that our limited abilities and various symptoms render us incapable of specific activities. We may welcome an offer of help with a challenging project, but sporadically, we might be determined to do it ourselves.

By keeping the focus of attention on our goals, we can dismiss unconstructive opinions (no matter how well intended) concerning our capabilities. Eyeing our intended targets and knowing we can achieve our destinations is as rewarding as it is stimulating. We can attempt to do things unassisted despite the simplicity or difficulty of particular challenges, which serves to strengthen our confidence. Achieving something without another's assistance and patting ourselves on the back for our accomplishment feels terrific.

I will maintain a reasonable goal
for my accomplishments.

December 25

Glory to God in the highest, and on earth peace, good will toward men.

—Luke 2:14

Peace is such a blessed condition. We could experience a reduction in grief if we chose peace over tension, suffering, and disharmony. Life can be harsh, cruel even. Sometimes it is easy to want to counter with words of discontent, but this cannot resolve any dilemmas or turn a situation of discord to one of bliss.

Turning strife into tolerance and indifference into love can help us maneuver the way to clearer, freer horizons as we gather up good intentions and kindness to cast about as a more fruitful alternative. When we are serene and loving toward others, this creates a gracious atmosphere, spilling over to all we encounter. When we render peace our anthem and love our cloak, we venture forth spreading good cheer.

I will rejoice
with peace and love for all humanity.

December 26

God gave us memory that we might have roses in December.

—Sir James M. Barrie

As a child, helping my mother plant sweet peas and snapdragons alongside the wild violets in our garden was a relished spring activity. After they began to bloom, I enjoyed picking a few flowers and pressing them inside my favorite books to enjoy at will, but I always left a few colorful blossoms for the bees and butterflies to weave through. My recollection of this favored spring project would carry me through the winter.

Our remembrances of events past and present are at times a shadow of what they previously were. On occasion, we might need assistance to remember. Retelling stories and events between family and friends and writing about chosen incidents in our journals are two activities that keep memories flourishing. The viewing of preferred photographs, alone or with a loved one, can elicit delightful moments to treasure, as can listening to another's memory of the favorable happenings. These can bolster our sporadic recall of special times while sparking smiles and much-needed laughter.

Within my memories, I choose to gaze beyond the weeds and pests,
concentrating instead on the beautiful
blossoms in the gardens of my life.

December 27

Do we not realize that self-respect comes with self-reliance?

—Abdul Kalam

There could be times when we are excessively fatigued and feel the need to lean on someone or something, literally or figuratively. We can achieve the healing benefits of self-reliance while also accepting help from family, friends, or assistive devices when it is crucial.

Adapting a healthy sense of dignity helps us attain a more independent lifestyle. If we settle for increased dependence, we may lose valuable self-assurance, which may be difficult to recover. One option that will boost our confidence is asking for help when necessary while continuing to engage in a moderate level of activity, enabling independence.

Observing those with disabilities living on their own can be encouraging to us. Our aim is to find poise when we require occasional assistance or when we go it alone, each contributing to a flourishing well-being. Developing healthy respect for ourselves will be an advantage that guides us through potential future years of health challenges.

My self-respect will blossom through my increased self-reliance.

December 28

Assertiveness is not what you do, it's who you are!
—Cal Le Mon

One valuable way those of us with medical problems can be assertive is in our wellness plans. We have a right to competent physicians and health care with respect. When we are visiting our primary care physicians, a time-saving technique is to arrive with a prepared listing of symptoms as well as any questions we may have, for it is better to inquire than to misunderstand. Next, we can follow through by receiving answers to our queries and noting these next to the correlating inquiry that may be of help afterward if fibro fog looms.

When we are proactive concerning our health and forming our wellness plans, we become our own health advocates through self-confident, constructive, healthy adjustments that promote decisiveness. When we traverse the scary waters of life, adopting a confident attitude can enable us to look and feel healthier.

I will develop a healthy, assertive attitude.

December 29

An inexhaustible good nature is one of the most precious
gifts of heaven, spreading itself like oil over the troubled
sea of thought, and keeping the mind smooth and equable
in the roughest water.

—Washington Irving

It can be a struggle to maintain a healthy, positive mood in the face of
fibromyalgia. Many a symptom might knock us off that place of good
standing as we land in the doldrums with ease.

If we have friends or family with upbeat personalities, we can consider
ourselves blessed. Despite our worst flare ups, merely conversing with these
cheerful people can help elevate our moods.

Being in the presence of a friendly person often lends a sense of calm
to troubling thoughts.

Even a telephone conversation can tend to smooth over and enliven
our day when we are engaged in the give-and-take with someone who
possesses a pleasant temperament. When we adopt them as role models,
their positivity can spread and envelop us. We can begin to soak up an
atmosphere of good cheer instead of focusing on our hardships. With this
beneficial inspiration, we can witness stress dissolving and smiles replacing
any frowns.

I will claim a good disposition
by releasing old attitudes.

December 30

Time is a sort of river of passing events, and strong is its current; no sooner is a thing brought to sight than it is swept by and another takes its place, and this too will be swept away.

—Marcus Aurelius

Even though the river of time is flowing at whatever stages we happen to be in our journeys, we can seek comfort by recalling the pleasant happenings in our lives. It can be gratifying to record the pleasing events in a journal and with photographs. When we need something comforting to cling to during the flood stage, these preserved moments are ours to revisit at will.

Whatever our current conditions, it can be reassuring to grasp that everything begins anew on the morrow. Life continues despite our actions. Despair can be swept away, replaced by joy and gratitude. Whenever we seem inundated with complications, we can bear in mind that tomorrow is twenty-four hours of fresh hopes sweeping away the high tides of life.

Today is a brand-new day.
I will make excellent use of it.

December 31

Hope rises like a phoenix from the ashes of shattered dreams.

—S. A. Sachs

Where is the youth whose dreams ruled the edge of night and hopes filled the tempestuous sky?

Is our creativity now obscured under the rigors of our obligations, with distress increasing and demands lining up around the corner? When did we last spend a day concentrating on precious dreams and opportunities, laced with delicate threads of hope?

As we orchestrate part of our day to be spent on free time and hobbies, we enhance our aspirations and creativity. When we clear the cobwebs from the dreamer—the hopeful within—we confront life with the serenity and calm that originates when we harness balance. When we relearn to hope if necessary, recalling how to dream, we eye the challenges waiting with wisdom and a resilient quantity of faith. And as we begin to gather our shattered hopes and dreams, we know that everything is as it should be.

I will gather my hopes
and dreams from obscurity.

Topic Index

G

H

I

J

K

L

M

N

O

Printed in the United States
by Baker & Taylor Publisher Services

Printed in the United States
by Baker & Taylor Publisher Services